Praise for

Legacy of Rescue: A Daughter's Tribute

The Holocaust and the Nazi era have been much written about. But you will find few with such a first-person feel, or so full of intriguing detail as the story Marta Fuchs tells here. *Legacy of Rescue* is about the experiences of her father, Morton (Miksa) Fuchs, and his family, as Jews in Nazi-era Hungary. Much of the story is first-person narrative, told by the people who survived these events.

As the title indicates, however, a major focus of the book is how Miksa survived, with assistance from a surprising quarter – the Hungarian (gentile) officer in charge of his forced labor battalion. Poignantly, Miksa Fuchs survived the war; his "rescuer" did not. The account of just how all this came about is a large part of what makes this book unique, and gripping reading. The example of heroism that the rescue demonstrates should stir us all, and especially provide a worthy model for young readers.

Another distinctive aspect of the book is the chapters devoted to Marta's follow-up to her father's story: her trips to Hungary to add to her knowledge of these events, and especially to honor Miksa's rescuer. The account of her meeting with this Hungarian army officer's son is one of the most moving passages in her Tribute.

It's not only the subject, but the style, that recommend *Legacy of Rescue.* It's full of detail, fascinating detail, and richly textured. Marta Fuchs has preserved her father's words as far as she feasibly could, translating them from Hungarian, with as little editing to smooth the narrative out as possible. This leaves the writing with a strong first-person flavor. At times it feels as if you can almost hear the old accents in the speech patterns of the protagonists!

To add another book to this already large body of literature requires considerable justification. Marta Fuchs has met that requirement well. You may think you have read everything you ever wanted to hear about this era; but you will find this book will stir you to tears, and inspire you with courage.

~ John F. Duge, PhD., MD, Retired Pastor, Central Seventh Day Adventist Church, San Francisco, CA

Like so many members of the Second Generation, Marta Fuchs grew up with a family fractured by the totalitarian regimes of the 20th century, its members scattered throughout the world. In her family of Hungarian Jews, the living members emigrated at different times: before and after the second world war; after the Hungarian Uprising of 1956. The dead lived on in stories and one of the most compelling was that of Zoltán Kubinyi. In this memoir, Marta Fuchs weaves his story and many others into her own search to document, commemorate and integrate the past and draw a portrait of a Righteous Christian in the Shoah.

~ Helen Epstein is the author of *Children of the Holocaust: Conversations with Sons and Daughters of Survivors* and the family and women's history *Where She Came From: A Daughter's Search for her Mother's History.*

www.helenepstein.com

As survivors, perpetrators, and witnesses of the Holocaust pass into history, Marta Fuchs' Legacy of Rescue: A Daughter's Tribute stands as a moving memorial to her parents, the extraordinary man who saved her father's life, and a farewell to a remarkable generation.

When someone is handed such a huge, traumatic inheritance, one must make meaning out of the horror and heroic stories of survival, or be engulfed by a tsunami of grief. Legacy of Rescue instills a battered yet resilient hope in the reader and a renewed belief in essential human goodness. The riveting and profoundly moving encounter between Marta and the son of the Righteous Gentile who risked his life to save her father is a testament to this spirit. Legacy of Rescue is an invaluable and heartfelt account of courage and determination in the face of overwhelming odds.

~ Armand Volkas, MFT, RDT, BCT is a psychotherapist who is the Director of Living Arts Counseling Center, Playback Theatre Ensemble, and Healing the Wounds of History Institute in the San Francisco Bay Area. His work focuses on cultural conflict transformation, collective trauma and social change. He conducts workshops internationally, including China, Japan, Singapore, Lebanon, Israel, Germany, and France. He is the son of Polish and Lithuanian Jewish Holocaust Survivors and Resistance Fighters.

http://www.livingartscenter.org/

We are not often aware of the enormous difference a single person can make in the lives of generations to come. Marta Fuchs' book, *Legacy of Rescue: A Daughter's Tribute,* which interweaves the author's voice with the voices of the generation before her and the generation after her, tells precisely that story in the context of her native Hungary in the years from the pre-Nazi era to the Communist era and into the present.

Fuchs was born in 1950 to Jewish parents in Tokaj, Hungary. Before her birth her father, born in 1911, had been consigned to a labor camp where many of his cohort died. He, too, might have died had it not been for the compassion and generosity of one man, his Commanding Officer, a devout Seventh Day Adventist. *Legacy of Rescue* describes the events of Fuchs' father's rescue by that man, Zoltán Kubinyi, culminating in the visit Fuchs made in 2011, with her brother and each of their two grown children (whose own reflections are included in the book), to Kubinyi's family in Hungary.

The pilgrimage made in this book is a pilgrimage into the author's past, narrated in order to preserve that past and allow it to inform the future. Passages in the voices of Fuchs' parents and aunts describe the effects of the Nazi era and then of the Communist period. Fuchs' family fled to the United States after the events of 1956, but maintained contact with Tokaj as a loved and vibrant home within them. The four American-born grandchildren feel, as a result, a deep sense of rootedness in the small Hungarian town.

This book is also the beautifully detailed story of the encounter of two men, Christian rescuer and Jewish survivor. Kubinyi, who was captured by the Russians and died of typhus in confinement, could not witness the results of his actions toward the Jews who were in his charge, but he is – thanks to the Fuchs' family's intervention – memorialized as a Righteous Gentile at Yad Vashem in Jerusalem.

A deeply moving moment in the book is Marta Fuchs' meeting with Kubinyi's son on the occasion of the 50th Anniversary Holocaust Commemoration in Tokaj when she spoke about his father. The elder Fuchs, Marta's father, who died in Pasadena in 2000, refused all his life to hate the Germans or the non-Jewish Hungarians, wanting instead to instill in those who knew him a compassion and perspective similar to the one that had been held by the man who saved his life. Granddaughter Sophie, in a beautiful passage toward the end of the book, writes of feeling the presence of the two men as she and her family sit in the Kubinyi home. How wonderful to think of them coming together to see the fruits of their lives' labor, the richness and depth of their children and grandchildren. Sophie points out, of course, that none of her family there would have been present without the actions of Kubinyi. Her gratitude is testament to both her grandfather, whose influence on those he loved was immense, and to the man who saved his life at the cost of his own.

Legacy of Rescue, though it centers on painful events, is finally a greatly uplifting book about the nobility to which human beings can rise in catastrophic moments. Both men, survivor and rescuer, stand as examples to us of the love we are capable of in the midst of horror and destruction. The book is written with deep authenticity and in exquisite prose.

~ Anita Barrows is a clinical psychologist and tenured professor at the Wright Institute, Berkeley. Four volumes of her poetry have been published, two of which have been granted national awards. She is also a translator from French, Italian, and German. Her most recent translations, in collaboration with Joanna Macy, are of the poetry and prose of Rainer Maria Rilke and have been published by Putnam and Harper Collins. She is a mother and grandmother and is descended from Hungarian Jews.

http://www.wi.edu/psyd-faculty-anita-barrows

All families have stories, some big and some small. Some fortunate families have a natural storyteller. Family history has the power to transform the individual, helping to explain one's life by filling and explaining the past. The power of one's own family story begs it to be told. Often the storyteller feels a calling to this very task.

Marta Fuchs' *Legacy of Rescue: A Daughter's Tribute* is that rare big story that reaches across timelines, across countries, and beyond one's individual family story and touches the human story.

In this global technological post 9/11 era, we use the term hero frequently. Marta shares this personal story of heroism from the past, richly describing the power of one man's actions. This inspirational message of hope, history, and legacy is a must read for adults and teens alike.

Legacy of Rescue: A Daughter's Tribute brings history to life, making the political personal, and helping us all reflect on ourselves.

This book is a vital resource for high school history and psychology courses.

This is a striking and compelling true story told by a gifted and chosen storyteller.

~ Jon Herzenberg, PsyD, is a San Francisco based clinical psychologist who works as family therapist with a specialty in teens. He is currently in his 10th year as Director of School Counseling at Drew School in San Francisco. In addition to his professional background, Dr. Herzenberg believes in the power of lived experience. He incorporates his experience as a black belt in Kung Fu San Soo, NCAA collegiate soccer player and high school coach, world traveler (previously residing in both China and Indonesia), avid gardener, son, brother, husband, and father. Dr. Herzenberg is also the cofounder of The Boys Project, a social emotional learning program for boys and schools.

http://drjonherzenberg.homestead.com

June 2015

To Michael Karish,

May you be inspired by the compassion and courage in these pages.

Mazel tov for winning the Fuchs Award!

Marla Fuchs

Also by Marta Fuchs (Winik)
with Henry Fuchs

Fragments of a Family: Remembering Hungary, the Holocaust, and Emigration to a New World

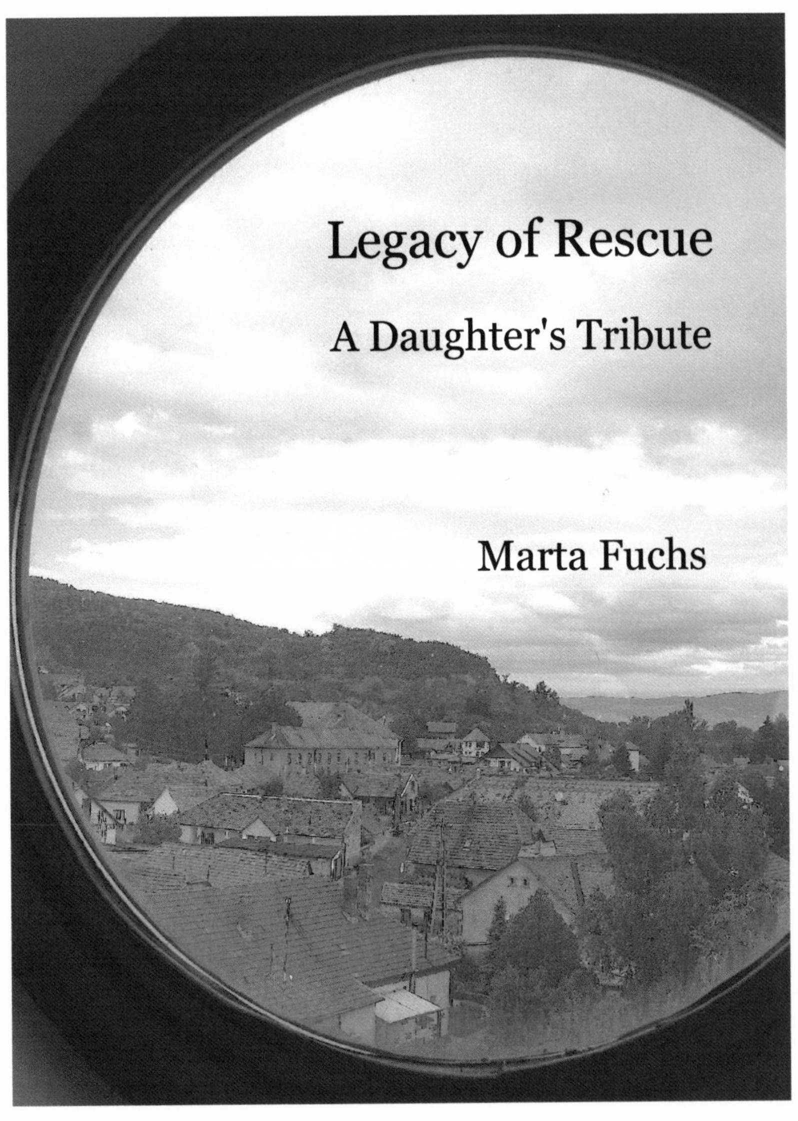
Legacy of Rescue
A Daughter's Tribute
Marta Fuchs

Családnak Press, Albany, CA

Front cover: Tokaj from top floor window of the Synagogue (Marta Fuchs, 2011)
Back cover: Miksa Fuchs with Marta, Tokaj, 1950

Portions of this book have appeared in the following publications: *Fragments of a Family: Remembering Hungary, the Holocaust, and Emigration to a New World; The California Therapist; The Christian Century; Spectrum; Martyrdom & Resistance; Oral History.*

Suggested Cataloguing:

Fuchs, Marta
Legacy of Rescue: A Daughter's Tribute / Marta Fuchs

Includes photographs and bibliographical references

ISBN 0-9778735-0-1

1. Holocaust, Jewish (1939-1945)—Hungary
2. Holocaust, Jewish (1939-1945)—Personal narratives
3. Righteous Gentiles in the Holocaust—Hungary
4. Children of Holocaust Survivors
5. Holocaust Survivors—United States—Biography
6. Hungary—History—Revolution, 1956—Personal narratives
6. World War, 1939-1945—Jews—Rescue
I. Title

940.53

In loving memory of my father

Morton (Miksa) Fuchs

(1911 – 2000)

and

To the courageous man who saved him

Zoltán Kubinyi

(1901 – 1946)

Table of Contents

1.	The bedtime story	p.1
2.	Prelude to war	p.4
3.	Labor camp and a prophecy	p.8
4.	Hearing fate of loved ones	p.11
5.	Encountering partisans, threat of decimation	p.18
6.	Order to be marched to Germany	p.24
7.	Liberation, Commanding Officer is captured	p.27
8.	Arriving home	p.35
9.	Jewish life in Tokaj after the war	p.58
10.	Mom and her sisters come back	p.61
11.	Getting married	p.65
12.	Life in Tokaj, 1948-1956	p.69
13.	Escaping, 1956	p.79
14.	Reflections	p.93
15.	Searching for Commanding Officer's name, honoring him as a Righteous Among the Nations	p.106
16.	Holocaust Commemoration, Tokaj, 1994	p.115
17.	Dad's letters from the hospital	p.128
18.	The last time I saw Dad	p.136
19.	Dad's passing and funeral	p.138
20.	Visiting the Kubinyis	p.147
21.	Memories of Grandpa	p.154
22.	The Tokaj Jewish cemetery	p.163

Epilogue	p.175
Fuchs and Billitzer Family family histories	p.177
Labor camp photograph notes	p.187
Recommended resources	p.188
Acknowledgments	p.190

1

The bedtime story

As children, my brother Henry and I only knew about one of Dad's experiences during the war. At bedtime in Hungary, he often told this story:

I had a friend in labor camp who smoked cigarettes. He asked me to keep his stash of tobacco for him and apportion it out to him so that it would last longer. In those days, you rolled the cigarettes yourself, so I would do that, putting some tobacco in these little papers, giving him one cigarette at a time. Well, as time went on, the stash of tobacco got smaller and smaller and I saw that pretty soon we would run out completely.

At that time, we were working in the forest in Russia cutting down trees, so there was a lot of sawdust on the ground. I thought to myself, why don't I start mixing in some of this sawdust to make the tobacco last longer? And pretty soon the cigarettes had more sawdust in them than tobacco. But my friend continued to smoke them, seemingly unaware of the difference.

Then the day finally arrived when there was no tobacco left at all and the cigarette I rolled for him was pure sawdust. As I handed it to him with great anticipation – what would he say? would he spit it out in disgust? – my friend started to smoke it, and after taking a few long breaths, inhaling and exhaling, he remarked with great gusto, "Miksa, this is the best cigarette I have ever had!"

We all roared with laughter, so hard that tears streamed down our faces, each and every time Dad told us this favorite tale. It would be three decades later in America that he would tell us in detail what happened to him during the five years he was in forced labor.

Hungarian Jews of military age were drafted in 1940 into forced labor battalions that were attached to the German-allied Hungarian army. Because of the anti-Jewish laws that had come into effect, they were no longer permitted to serve in the regular army, but had to fulfill required military obligations in these labor battalions. Working first in Hungary then in the Ukraine, they were generally treated with cruelty. Many died from brutality, malnutrition, and disease.

Dad was one of the lucky few to survive, and it was because of the extraordinary man who was his Commanding Officer in the final year of the war. This is a tribute to them both, men of compassion and courage who made a difference.

The words of my father who begins this book, and also of my mother and two of her sisters, are my translations of their original testimonies in Hungarian. Their extensive descriptions of life in Hungary before, during, and after the Holocaust can be found in *Fragments of a Family: Remembering Hungary, the Holocaust, and Emigration to a New World* (c1997) which I wrote with my brother Henry Fuchs.

2

Prelude to war

In the '30's, the newspapers wrote about the rise of Hitler and that anti-Semitic activities were going on in Germany and later in Austria. We had no radio at home but we read the newspaper daily. And during family gatherings, such as on Saturday afternoons and holidays, and also daily when I went to the Temple, we discussed with friends the newspaper articles and whatever anyone had heard from other people. With great worry we were anxiously watching what was going to happen.

I was working for the Steiner Company, a Budapest chocolate and gourmet desserts company, as a traveling salesman. When the Jewish laws came into effect in 1938, I had to have a front, a straw man under whose name I could work. There was a retired Major, an old man in his 70's, who had a license to sell various things. He was a very nice and fine old man. His name was Lukovics. He would get 10 percent of my earnings. In the bank we drew up papers to this effect. All papers would go to him in Ungvár, near Kassa, and he would send them to me in Tokaj. After a while he wanted 15 percent.

Dad, 1931

My sister Ilonka and her husband Samu Katz lived next to their store in Vásárosnamény. Everyone there had a maid. Once when I was visiting, the maid rushes in saying, "Katz *Úr*, please come! The volunteer corps broke into the store!" So I go down with my brother-in-law. The store's door is broken, it's wide open, and there are about 20 of these volunteer corps boys and they are seizing the leather coats. They went in and in the name of the nation they commandeered them. They were nice leather coats and they all tried them on and simply left with them.

Well, I was just watching with amazement. As one of these young men is putting a coat on and is about to go out with it, I grabbed him and said, "You won't take this out!" I pulled the coat off him and threw him out. He was scared and left. My brother-in-law turns to me, "What are you doing?! What are you doing?! Leave him! Let him take it!" I just couldn't stand it. They emptied the store and took an enormous amount of leather coats, about 50 of them, and nothing could be done. We put what remained in order and fixed the door from the inside.

There were no laws, nothing. Jews didn't have the rights for anything. And if you complained, you would have gotten in jail. The laws did not protect Jews at all at that time.

There was also the case that these same people took some kind of merchandise from the grocery store and the Jewish owner went to the police. They sat him down saying that "Tomorrow we will listen to you, you'll tell us your problem," and then they threw him out since he complained. So it wasn't possible that they would protect your house or your business. There weren't any laws. They beat up the Jews.

At the same time, the day before, I was in the Temple

with my brother-in-law. And as we're coming out of the Temple, there stand two policemen and they arrested every stranger. And I, too, was considered a stranger. My brother-in-law knew the policemen and said, "Look, this is my brother-in-law. He is here because he came to my house for the holidays!" "No, no, you must come in."

So they took me in and locked me in jail with other guests I had seen in the Temple, a father or sibling who came to visit for the holidays so that they should be together. It was already late at night when somehow they let us free, how I don't know, only that they let us go. And the next day this happened in the store, that they broke in.

I don't remember that in Tokaj there was this kind of thing. Tokaj is not a border city and there weren't any of these volunteer corps there. These were border cities; about a half-hour walk was the Romanian border. In Tokaj, Jews and non-Jews lived peacefully together. Some non-Jews didn't patronize the Jewish stores, but they were not anti-Semitic openly. In Tokaj there wasn't such a thing.

3

Labor camp and a prophecy

Dad's markings, top row: #1 is his brother Vilmos, #2 is Dad.

I was called up in May of 1940. My first labor camp group I was in for several months was in the Bacska region, the village of Szond. My brother Vilmos was in the same group. The majority of the boys were from Tokaj. Then they discharged us and a few weeks later we got called back in and another group was formed.

Most of us accepted our fate, but there was a Berkowits boy, I can't recall his first name, who finished school and was in my first group. He was a young man, so he probably went to another group afterwards but later died somewhere. He was a very unusual boy, an intelligent, learned boy, except he felt the full weight of the uncertainty of our situation. He never accepted it, never did the work unless the guards were there. He would say, "This is an injustice to have to work just because we're Jewish." This was in contrast to those of us who accepted our fate in the labor camp.

There was another Tokaj boy with us, Bernát Baldinger. Once we were in a place called Nagybocskó, which between the wars was Hungary again. Everyday we went up to the mountains. There was a big forest there where we cut and cleaned the logs, and there was a little river we put the logs in to be brought down and taken to build things at the front. Sundays we didn't work and sometimes we got day passes.

The Tisza River was at Nagybocsko and the Maramarossziget, the isle, was across the river on the other side. One day we heard that the Belzi Rabbi was there. He was known as a *csoda* rabbi, a "miracle rabbi."

About six or eight of us went to see him. There were a lot of people there. We went over to the *gabbai*, the assistant, who was letting people into a private place. The *gabbai* said only four men could go in, so I wasn't able to go. Bernát Baldinger was one who went in. As they entered, the rabbi right away looked at Bernát and said, "You will no longer to be a labor camp worker. Soon all of you will be discharged, and you" pointing to Bernát, "won't be a labor camp worker anymore."

The entire labor camp group was discharged in 1940 and we all went back to Tokaj. About one or two weeks later on a Sunday morning, I was traveling by train to Budapest on some business. The train starts up and suddenly stops. There is a lot of noise, people are screaming. Everyone gets off. We see a big crowd and someone said that Bernát was hit by the train. He had been rushing to catch it, started to jump on, and the train cut him in two.

I became ill. We had been together in labor camp. He was older than me, about 32 years old. Of course, I didn't end up going to Budapest. The next day was his funeral. Everyone was crying. It was a big funeral. The coffin was carried on a stretcher and was taken to the Temple. The rabbi gave a speech either at the Temple or at the cemetery. Four people carried the coffin on their shoulders. We four who were with him in labor camp carried him first, then others took turns after us.

I don't understand this -- that the *csoda* rabbi somehow saw this? He pointed only to Bernát Baldinger.

4

Hearing fate of loved ones

We were somewhere in Russia in the Bryansk Forest in 1944. For years we had not received any news from home regarding what is happening with our loved ones. The guards who were with us went home periodically for vacation and when they came back they are saying that everywhere the Jews were picked up and they locked them in ghettos, and they took a lot of them to Germany.

They mentioned Auschwitz and there in the gas chambers they then exterminate the Jews. At first we didn't want to believe it. What we thought was that they were just telling us this out of wickedness, to give us heartache.

We were working in the forest harvesting trees and packing the big trees onto the wagons at the railway station. One day a train came in full of Hungarian soldiers who were coming back from vacation and were returning to the front, and they said the same thing as our guards. If they, too, are saying this, then it must be true. They were speaking about horrible things, that this happened in this city and it happened like this and it happened like that. Then we saw already that this is true. But even then we didn't want to believe it.

Unbelievable! We didn't believe it. We thought maybe to a couple of people, maybe some hostages they took. But everyone? The fact that the children, little children, women they would kill, send to the gas? We thought that perhaps the Jews who are not trustworthy they took out of circulation and they situated them up there and they will set them free after the war. But that they will kill them? Why? It's unbelievable!

Spring 1944

Mom (Ilona, Ica)
26 years old

And then we arrived in Auschwitz. By this time it was daylight, and on the other side of the fence I saw people in striped pajamas, in long gowns and nightgowns, and no hair. We didn't know if they were Jews or not, and we think that this is the crazy sanatorium. We didn't know that a half an hour later we'll be there, too. We were told to throw down our packages we had worked so hard to put together to take with us. Women and men were told to stand in separate lines. I remember wearing a shawl.

Mengele – I can still see him. If I could draw, I could draw you a picture of him, that blond haired man, so I see him in front of me. He stood there, "left and right," and I wanted to put on my mother the shawl since she was going in the other line and I wanted to say goodbye. Mengele said, "*Brach nicht grussen Abend Werde ziezamen stetten,*" "You'll see each other later, no need to say goodbye."

Then we arrive at the building and they ask who can speak German. Löwy *néni,* who we went through the entire time with, spoke German and also we knew a little bit of German. They said, "Undress, hold your glasses, carry your shoes in your hands and put them in the liquid." They pushed us naked in one room with men gaping at us. Then German men shaved us everywhere. They cut your hair, they cut the underarm, they cut you below, and pushed you into the other room, "Hold your arms up."

In the other room they put the shower on us. We hit

each other in the chaos, could you imagine? Everybody was yelling. Then "rush rush rush" we went out the other side of the room and they gave you some *schmate*, some rags, nightgowns, old dresses, whatever they grabbed, "Put it on!" and we find ourselves with these people who we think are crazy. We were cold and thirsty and the Germans said, "Don't drink the water," that the water was not good to drink. Everybody was so thirsty and everybody just looked at each other, "What happened?"

Then all of a sudden from one of the barracks somebody yelled my name. Gyula Wassermann it was, in striped pajamas, and he gives me a handkerchief because his sister was with us and he must have heard what happened with us, to tie on her shaven head. And he gives a piece of bread that we ate, twelve of us. His sister Dusika was with us in Auschwitz continually. And what was the name of that daughter, she was so young, who lived there at the Wassermanns? There were two young girls there. Rozenberg was their name. One was with us in our bunker.

Then again "rush rush rush" and they took us to the C *láger*, 19 block. The C *láger* was the extermination camp. Everyday from here they selected the weak, naked, to go to the crematorium. We weren't worth so much that they put a number on us, like later on we met people who had numbers, like in the B *láger*, people worth it for working and therefore they gave them numbers. But everyday they selected from us to the crematorium. We just smelled all the smoke.

Sárika (Pityu)
22 years old

Mom's younger sister

And then we arrived at dawn, the drums sounded, it was light, to Auschwitz. "*Schnell schnell schnell*", rush rush rush and the Germans were already standing there with their dogs, and then Mother and Father got off. We had a blue shawl with embroidery on the edges and Ica put that on mother's shoulders. There was a sign that said, "With work you are free." Then we saw that they had already taken Father and Mother to the other side. Never again did we see them. But we didn't know yet what will happen.

And we saw that there were people fenced off behind a tall, barbed wire fence, bald. Well, what we thought was that those who are sick, the crazy ones, are also kept here. We didn't know that by the next day we, too, would look like that.

Then they put us in lines and we had to take everything off. Imagine what I was feeling, that I had a sanitary pad on. And then that German, of course I had to throw this pad down, shaved my head. The German soldier, boy soldier, shaved my head, under my arms, and then he yelled at me "*schwein rein*," clean as a pig.

But before it was my turn, Gyula's sister had some photographs with her and she gave them to me, that I should put them between the pads, because clean cotton pads I still had in the ghetto and in the cattle cars could still bring them with me and I somehow was able to change them. So between two pads I put the photographs so they didn't show. But I had to throw them down.

And when he shaved me, well imagine, a young girl,

having to undress in front of a man, and that you're menstruating. It was the most humiliating thing in my life. As long as I live I won't be able to forget it, because you can't forget that.

And when I was finished, I wanted to put the pads back on so that I should save the photographs, but then again he yelled at me "*schnell schnell*" and of course I proceeded in the line. We went on -- Ica, Bözsi, and the rest who were together with us in a group -- totally naked.

Bözsi
30 years old

Mom's older sister

What we thought, because that's what he heard, was that families will stay together and that they are taking us to work. Father was a 62 year old young man. There he didn't count as a young person, but he was a 62 year old, strong, energetic, and Mother also.

So, when we are getting off, they quickly put Mother this way. This royal blue shawl was on her shoulder, I can still see it, and Father was standing here, they put him there. And Tokaj families we knew, with young women and children, they put next to Mother. We thought that if they needed help with something, these people would help them.

I wanted to run over there to kiss her. I got the first slap then, it cut me so, a German hit me so hard. I was next to Ica, she and Sárika didn't even notice because everything was happening so quickly and turbulently that no one knew what is really happening. The ones who had children, a young woman even 20 or 30 years old she was,

was taking a child, holding hands, and they took them that way, to the left side. You never knew whether the left side or the right side is good.

And we went in there and right away you had to take off your clothes, hold your shoes in your hand, and there was a kind of Clorox water that you had to dip it in. They cut our hair as if they shaved you, as smooth as your palm that's how it became, and they shaved your private parts and under your arms.

Then there was Mengele and this kind of German woman, I don't even know what they called her. Such a tall, terrible, really an earthly species of Satan, an evil person. She was so horrible. Everyone, if she saw them, she whipped thoroughly with the dog whip.

Then they took us into a room, there were more of us there, I don't know how many hundred, and we just stood there. Nothing for 48 hours, for two days. You couldn't even go out to finish your business, nothing at all. And they didn't give us anything at all to eat. Many people already went crazy or they died there, because you couldn't take a breath and you didn't eat. In that room for two days we remained.

And then I asked one of the female guards, "Where are our parents? When am I going to see them?" She said, "Look outside, they are going up in smoke there," that they are coming out of the chimney there. I thought that I would kill her.

Standing (left to right): Bözsi, Sárika, Ilona (Mom), Renée (not pictured is 2nd oldest Margit who had already left for America; Renée , the oldest, would soon follow)

Sitting: Flora Szász and Salamon Engel (both born in 1880)

Kistokaj, 1937

5

Encountering partisans, threat of decimation, new Commanding Officer arrives

Group portrait of Jewish partisans in the forest.circa 1941 – 1944, unknown locale, U.S. Holocaust Memorial Museum, courtesy of Benjamin (Miedzyrzecki) Meed

Deep within the Bryansk Forest where we were working there were partisans. I didn't encounter even one, but many among the boys who went in deeper did. They were boys from beneath the Karpat who spoke Slovak. And the partisans said to them, "Come over to us. All this is true. They took the Jews away and they killed them in Germany in the concentration camps, in the gas chambers they kill them. And you have nothing to wait for here. All of you come over. During the night you should attack the guards, take the weapons away from them, kill them. Break into the arsenal and gather together the weapons and come into the forest and there we will be waiting for you."

The boys were seriously considering this. Now then, a group who was thinking reasonably said, "Here are these old Hungarian soldiers, our guards, who are in the same *tsuris*, predicament as us. And you see, they weren't bad to us, and we should kill them? You cannot consider killing them. And there are here with us these older, weaker Jewish men who cannot run or what. We should leave them here?" So there were more reasonable ones. I was among them, the larger side that didn't want to kill anyone and I worked hard against it.

So we decided that we would stand guard all night. We would be careful that these people wouldn't do anything, and we discussed what should be done. What we said was those who want to go should go. "You don't need to kill anyone, just go."

The next day they sent some men in three wagons to central supplies to buy food for us and hay and oats for the horses. There were wagons for the squadron, six or eight wagons, and about ten or twelve horses. You needed to get supplies for 200 men and also when we were changing locations. And these men never came back. They went into the forest and went over to the partisans. The following day we went out to work and 20 men didn't come back. All of them went over to the partisans. The next day again about 20-25 men disappeared.

We had then a Commanding Officer who you couldn't say was bad, but he wasn't good either. He didn't do us any favors but he didn't do bad things either. He was an elderly man and so bitter. He had to be there and be responsible for everything. And he said, "This cannot continue like this any longer."

He said he will lock up the entire area. At the time, we were put up on this farm in the stables. He said, "No one can leave the area." He will go into Gommel, the Headquarters, and report this. "And you know what this will mean. There will be decimation here. Be prepared for it. There will be decimation." Decimation is that they line up the men in a row, 1, 2, 3, 4, and 10, boom boom boom.

They shoot him. This had happened, so this can happen again. They kill every tenth man and we were prepared for this.

In the morning, the Commanding Officer left in a carriage, a horse and buggy, with the driver and the Commanding Officer's assistant, both Jewish boys. Every officer had his own aide, called his "young man" who took care of his boots, cleaned his clothes, and took care of his things. So they went in to Headquarters.

On the road a car came toward them, the horses got frightened and suddenly reared and bolted. The carriage turned over, fell into the ditch, and the leg of the Commanding Officer broke. Nothing happened to the two Jewish boys, the driver and the aide. They both just fell into the ditch.

Well, what can be done? They right away took him directly to the hospital in Gommel and from there they went to Headquarters to report what happened. Of course, the boys didn't say why the Commanding Officer was coming in, only that this and this happened. Well, of course they will send out another Commanding Officer.

And we all day were locked up there in the camp. We weren't allowed to go out and we were trembling so much that when they come back, who would be the tenth one here? All day, you can imagine, it was like this.

Finally, the wagon arrives and we saw that an unfamiliar officer gets off. Immediately he gathers us together, asking everyone to come. We encircled him and he related what had happened, that they had taken our Commanding Officer to the hospital because the wagon turned over and his leg broke. "And they sent me out in place of him and now I will be your Commanding Officer. I heard what happened here in this camp. I ask you very much, please no one escape anymore because that just causes trouble for the rest, and for those of you, too, who go into uncertainty. Everyone stay here and I will look after you and guarantee that no harm will come to you." So this was a very fine man. He was a Seventh Day Adventist.

So the days and weeks went on and we went out to work and he really took care of everything for us and everything was very nice. It was very good after this in the camp.

And there was someone, my friend Isaac Guttman. He was this short, little, sickly boy. He was very weak constitutionally but a great scholar, very educated, and he was very educated in Judaism also. Someone called the Commanding Officer's attention to this boy, that he is weak physically. He hardly ate anything because he was strictly kosher. He only ate bread and jam and margarine and lived on this for years. I always took care of him, watched out for him, because he was a Tokaj boy. I remember when we left, his mother accompanied us to the station and took my hand, "Watch out for my child!" So I took care of her child and watched out for him very carefully. That was in 1940. I was 29 and he was 26, 27.

So, the Commanding Officer appointed him to be the camp rabbi and he didn't have to go out to work. Instead, once on Sunday or Saturday, he had to deliver a speech. He very nicely prepared it and quoted something from the Torah and spoke to us about that in Hungarian. This was the extent of his duties, the camp clergyman he was. So this Commanding Officer was such a fine man.

Like also when somebody was smoking on Saturday, he would say, "Why are you smoking Saturday? This is forbidden by your religion to be smoking on Saturday." And if his boots were there in the workshop to be repaired, if they weren't ready on Friday, he sent his servant to bring them back because he didn't want Jews to work on his boots on Saturday.

Or when before Yom Kippur, he went to the German headquarters we were working for there, that this day they should give us off because this is the biggest holiday for the Jews, Yom Kippur. Of course, they didn't, so we had to go out.

He came with us and all day he was with us. He didn't eat anything either, only a glass of water, nothing. And in the evening when we came home from work, he left us so we could pray, and he gave a double portion of food to everyone because all day we were fasting, not everyone, but the majority. So he was such a decent man like this.

It also happened once that somewhere on the edge of a forest we were lodged, and it was announced that you couldn't go out of the forest because suddenly enemy planes could come and see that men are moving here and then they would bomb. We had to watch out for this.

Now then, there next to the forest, a few meters away, was a little river, and two buddies and I went out there to the river's edge and washed clothes. It was a Sunday afternoon, there was no work, and so we washed our clothes and ourselves.

And immediately a guard came over and yelled, "You have violated the order! Come over to the Commanding Officer and report that you have violated the order! You were told that you shouldn't go out and you went out here to the river!"

The Commanding Officer sent the guard away and said to us, "Look, the reason I gave this order was to be careful for your lives. Here up high, enemy planes can come. You can't even hear them. If they see that men are moving here, then they will bomb here. Your own lives you were risking. Don't do this kind of thing anymore! Now go back and don't leave the forest!"

The new Commanding Officer

Russia, 1944

6

Order to be marched to Germany

All of a sudden word came that the Germans are retreating because the Russians are pressing forward and always the Germans and we were behind them. We worked behind the front. We cut trees out in the forest and cleaned off the long trees and put them on trains and the trains took them out to the front. With them they built these kinds of forests, bunkers, protective things behind which they fought. Or we built roads, or for the railroads we put down rails or removed them, repaired them. Or on the road we broke up rocks and everything. It was hard work.

And the order came that we were to be taken out to Germany to be given over to the Germans. It was given in writing, that this group of Jews should be taken to Germany because they are retreating, daily coming closer and closer, and there is no longer any need for the work if they are not fighting. Well, you see, they didn't know what to do anymore but take our group out to Germany and hand them over to the Germans, to the concentration camp. With many they did this. This was in the beginning of 1945, I think. I don't know exactly.

The Jewish boys who worked in the office knew about everything since this Commanding Officer was very candid and told the men what the order was. "Don't be afraid," he said. We won't go to Germany."

So we started out by foot and walked for days. I don't know how many hours we went, comfortably, several times we rested. And everywhere there were these army storehouses of food since everywhere there were German and Hungarian soldiers. For every group, every squadron, there were food storehouses. So our Commanding Officer purchased provisions for us and we were well taken care of on the road. In fact, we were never taken care of so well anywhere.

And we didn't go to Germany. Instead, he took us to Hungarian headquarters in Kassa. He didn't say what the order was, that we were to be sent to Germany. Instead, he said that we were sent back because they are retreating, and here we are, he wishes to turn in this group. They said they couldn't take us but that he should take us out to Germany and give us over to the Germans in the concentration camp.

We were there for about two, three days, in barracks at an army post, a military base. It was empty because every soldier was out at the front. They put us up in the basement, not on top. Everyone had a blanket and on that and hay they could sleep.

And there we saw that the walls were bloody. They tortured men there. We didn't see the torture, just the aftermath. Everywhere there were these blood clots, so bloody were the walls and the rocks and everything.

We worked cleaning up the grounds. I swept the walkways in front of the house with two or three other boys.

Then from here we started out toward Hungary. We went for about two days, and there in the vicinity of Miskolc we arrived at a farm. There were about 140-160 of us maybe, because the rest had escaped to the partisans. Our Commanding Officer went in to the owner but he wasn't there. Only an old man and his wife and maybe two older women were there. The young ones were all soldiers or were in some kind of service. He offered that we work there on the farm because there weren't any workers who would harvest the corn and the potatoes and wheat. Everything that was out in the fields was already ripe and needed to be harvested. They needed to be gathered up, put in bags, the wheat taken to the mill, the potatoes put down in the cellar, and the corn put up on the bench and cleaned. We would undertake this kind of work and in exchange they would feed us.

So we were very happy. They placed us in this big storehouse which was empty. We went out in the morning to the fields, collected the potatoes and the corn in bags, onto the bench, down to the cellar, to here and there. They gave us a sheep they killed, or a calf, and the men ate that. And from the flour we baked bread, and potatoes and other food they also gave us. And there we were hidden, for about ten days or two weeks.

All of a sudden, we are coming home from work and there are six military policemen there. Someone had reported us, that Jews are hiding here. These were special military men who picked up the escaped soldiers, and they came to arrest us. Our Commanding Officer made it clear to them that there is an order to take us out to Germany and that we were resting up here. We are working to help out the farmers and because we are in need of food.

Well, we couldn't leave the area and needed to pack up, and the next morning we started out toward Germany with these six military policemen accompanying us. We went by foot until evening where we ended up somewhere on a farm and rested, and in the morning we continued. It went on like this for a couple of days.

Suddenly in the middle of the night, we awoke to some movements. We were sleeping, all 140 of us, in a big barn where food for the animals was kept. Our Commanding Officer had come in and woke up a few of the men. "You should be quiet, get dressed, we are leaving now." They in turn passed the word to wake everyone else. They told us briefly that our guards, probably under our Commanding Officer's orders, had gotten these military policemen drunk and they are lying there sleeping, and we are now going to escape. And we then in the middle of the night quickly running escaped in another direction from what was the original one. For two or three days we escaped, always spent the night somewhere, went further, and we reached a large city, Balassagyarmát.

7

Liberation, Commanding Officer is captured

Balassagyarmát, *A "Legbátrabb város"*
Civitas Fortissima | Szent Korona Rádió
("The Bravest city")

In Balassagyarmát, we heard shooting and bombs exploding. Soldiers were coming back from the front on horseback and on foot. In the entire city far away you could see the cannon fire. We could therefore see that here is the war.

Our Commanding Officer arranged for us to be put up in cellars with the civilians. About 50-60 men in this cellar, 50-60 men in that cellar, because the entire city was in the cellar since they were bombing. There weren't any Jews there, only us. There were old women and old men. Young people were nowhere to be seen. They were all at war. And all day, these old people flung their crosses and prayed loudly while we just sat there.

All of a sudden, a young woman with a little girl appears. The little girl must have been 4 or 5 and was very badly thin, worn, ragged. The young woman came over to us, "Your are Jews, right?" She could see that, of course. We had yellow armbands and on them was the number of the squadron, 108/52. "I am Jewish, too, and I am hiding in the vicinity here. If you could help at all, we are hungry." Well, of course. She was happy, everyone was. What bread we could give her and whatever else, butter or jam, we gave her. She told us what had happened there and of course we helped her out.

No one slept at all in the cellar because we heard the loud noises. Bombs struck here and there. And when it was light, we heard some unfamiliar commando sounds in the yard.

We climbed out from the cellar and there we see a bunch of Russian soldiers. That was the first time in my life that I saw Russian soldiers. They looked so unshaven, for days they hadn't shaved, and they had rifles. We put our hands up and they saw the armbands on us. The civilians didn't dare to come up; they were afraid. We asked the soldiers what the situation was and they received us in a very friendly manner. Many of our boys could speak Russian with them. The soldiers said that we should stay here and they continued on further.

Suddenly, some other boys from our squadron come and they bring over this kind of halom bread, a long square kind of bread. They said, "Here in the other squadron is a bakery and the Germans were baking bread all night and they are leaving and they left everything there." Everyone ends up going over there and we couldn't believe seeing so much bread! We all took about five or six loaves, tucking them here, tucking them there, and though we had to be sparing so that there would be some left for tomorrow, we ate ate ate!

The Russians came back in the afternoon and they gathered us up on this big square. Well, hungry we were not because we had plenty of bread. That German bread was so delicious.

Everywhere in the city Hungarian soldiers who had escaped, and the labor camp workers, were all in hiding. And now all of them came out. All the soldiers had changed into civilian clothes they had bought.

Meanwhile, a group of us encircled our Commanding Officer and pleaded with him, "*Hadnagy Úr*, Second Lieutenant, Sir, please change your clothes, here are the Russians!" "No, no, no, no, no," he said. "I will not. I haven't done anything wrong. I have nothing to be ashamed of. I am proud to have saved the lives of you men. I am an honorable member of the Hungarian Officer Corp. I am proud to be a member of the Hungarian Army. Nothing will happen to me."

As the Russian soldiers came to arrest him, we pleaded with them as well, protesting, "This is a good man! He saved our lives!" They would not listen and took him away.

Our Commanding Officer wasn't familiar with the Russians. He was such a straight thinking person. He knew he did good, only good with the men. He saved our lives and he thought the Russians will accept that.

But with the Russians there isn't logic. They put someone in prison and he is there for years until they interrogate him. This is the system with the Russians. And here he is in army uniform. That represents the enemy. It didn't matter that you talked with them because they didn't even listen.

So then we were in a big group and those in soldier's uniform were put in one group, civilians in another. They put us in a line and if they found on someone some money, they took it. Well, what kind of money did they find on us? They found zlotys, Polish coins, because the last time that's what we got in Rollni, but it could only have been for 10 days, the equivalent of one or two dollars, and there wasn't anything to spend it on. So there were a lot of zlotys on everyone and the Russians took all of that. And if someone had a watch, they took that away, taking the watches off people's arms. Now then, I see this, so I took mine off and tucked it in the back of my pants and was able to save it. They searched me thoroughly, no watch, and went on to the next person.

Then they took away those in soldier's uniform including our Commanding Officer, our guards, and all the military police. We didn't hear what happened to them afterwards.

They took the civilians and us to Hatvan. I don't remember how long we walked, a day or so. In Hatvan is a big sugar factory directly next to the train station, and there in a small room they crammed us all in. We couldn't sit down except by squeezing closely together, and we couldn't even lie down on the floor. We mostly could only lean against the wall. We were like this all night, locked in, with two Russian soldiers at the door.

And what did they give us to eat? They put in a pale of water and brought in one bread for three or four men. And there was this kind of tomato paste, this five kilo, ten pound ketchup in a box. We ate it with the bread and we drank the water. If someone had to go out to the WC, then he knocked on the door and the guard went out with him and brought him back.

In the morning, they took us to a school building a few blocks away and told us we should wait there. "Everyone will get a document and with that he could go home. Wherever he wants to go, he can."

We were standing there for a couple of hours and all of a sudden, Russian soldiers arrived again and grabbed us and other men. We were six of us in a group and in that six was that little man who was our camp rabbi, my good friend from Tokaj, Isaac Guttman. And they took us all to the sugar factory.

Trains arrived there and on them in crates and sacks were provisions which needed to be taken off. We had to carry them on our backs for a good distance and take them into a warehouse. We did this all day. In the evening, they locked us in this little place, and again in the morning we worked. This went on for three days. When are we going to be set free from here? Among us there was someone who could speak Russian. "One or two days more, one or two days more still," the Russians told us.

It then occurred to one of the boys that we need to escape from here. But how? This was a big yard, fenced in all around, and by the gate there were guards, Russian soldiers with rifles. Someone noticed that in one of the corners there was a stretcher leaning against one of the houses. He thought that we should lay down one of our boys on it and wrap his head and arms up with the towels that each of us had. This friend of mine, Isaac Guttman, was the lightest and smallest. So we wrapped up his head and arms and smeared the tomato paste on him. We banged on the door, "Help! Help!" The guards opened it, saw that he is injured, and we ran out to the gate, all of us carrying him. We run with the stretcher for about a block, we turn, he gets off and takes off his "bandages," and we run back to our lodging.

"Well, what's going on that you came back?" they asked us. Because others came back but the Jews had not. And then we wait and wait and hear that many had already left. Those who had worked had gotten that document and left.

Somebody thought we should go to that office in the area where the Russian officers were writing the documents so that people could leave. On that document was that kind of three-cornered Russian stamp. One of our boys goes there, the Jewish boy who spoke Russian, to say that here we are a group. He did not say that we had escaped, but that for three days we had worked here. And we got the documents. All of us, four or five of us who were from Tokaj, and one who was not. This was in the evening and the next morning we started walking, leaving Hatvan.

Now then, how did we eat? The bread had run out and we didn't get any food. No one was seeing after us. We just went like this, walking on the main road, and where there was a farm we asked there. They gave us potatoes or some bread or something and we ate that. And there in the stables we slept and drank water, and in the morning we went further.

We went on the road like this for about three days when all of a sudden we see far off a big group coming toward us with Russian soldiers surrounding it. Immediately we realize that they are gathering together civilians from the streets or from homes, and they are taking them away to work for the Russian military needs.

We quickly got off the road and hid in the bushes. One of the boys noticed that those men who were originally with us in our unit, who were let free the previous day, were there in that group. These Russian soldiers took many of them out to Russia and many did not come back.

We continued walking, perhaps for a week or so. Somewhere we went up on a train where there were Russian soldiers, and they were so good to us. They gave us something to eat. We were very hungry. Back on the road walking, when there wasn't a farmhouse, we knocked at a house and said, "We are hungry" and they gave us something, bread or potatoes or milk, something. Like this we begged. We were hungry.

At some station we got on a train that went until Nyiregyháza. When we arrived, we encountered Jewish boys who had come back from another labor camp and were waiting at the station for other Jewish boys to come back. They told us that there is a house where we could rest up and be fed. A kitchen had been set up where they were cooking. And what did they cook? Potatoes. That's it, potatoes. We got some bread and perhaps milk if they could find some, and maybe onions and fruit. This was it.

There were about 10-15 men there, all of them tired, broken down, as they came back from the labor camps, and they rested there for a couple of days and went further on. And always those who had stayed there already for a couple days cooked. I don't know who supplied the food, where it came from. I, too, for a few days cooked there with the other boys.

One of our boys who wanted to go be a workman I accompanied with Sanyi Frankel to the train station to see to it that he finds some train or some group with whom he could go. We took him out and, in fact, he found some group that he went with.

As we are coming back from the station, walking there in Nyiregyháza, we turn at one of the corners and we run into one of the groups that two Russian soldiers were gathering up. We turn around and run away. "Hey!" and one of them drew his rifle on us. Well, of course we stopped and they came over. Now then, what's going to happen? Where are we going?

They took us in a group, about 50-60 people, women, men, all young people, civilians. Only the two of us were Jews. Again they picked civilians from the streets or homes. With the Russians it didn't matter if you cried, "Here is my little child!" or "I am sick" or anything. It didn't interest them, they didn't listen, just "Let's go!" We were taken to some barracks and divided into different groups, you do this, you do that.

And again, with Sanyi Frankel and about two or three more men, young people who are able to do some work, we had to carry sacks of flour from one warehouse to another. Not on a cart but instead two men would pick it up. We did this until evening but they gave us very good things to eat like some kind of potato soup. It was very greasy but it was so delicious. Well, we were also hungry. And there were plenty of potatoes in it. There wasn't any meat in it, only potatoes. And they gave us bread, a big piece of bread that was very delicious. And there were these sacks with prunes which we cut open and all day ate the prunes. It went like this for three days. When we finished the work, they kicked us out, "Go!"

We went back to our lodgings and they were happy to see us. "We were wondering where you are, because it goes like this here, that they gather up the people, everyone escapes, and they gather them up again."

So we rested up and the next day we started out for Tokaj. This was in January 1945, I think.

8

Arriving home

Tokaj, Bethlen Gábor utca (the main street)

We arrived home sometime in the beginning of February. I don't remember exactly. We arrived at night and there was a lot of snow. We come into the city and we meet some people who recognized us. They were very surprised. "*Jaj*, Fuchs *Úr*! Well, where did you come from, where? And Mr. Frankel!" who was also with me. So I answer and then ask, "Did some other Jews come home?" They say, "Of course, they are here, they are at Mrs. Dudás. Mr. Wassermann and Ernö Mandel and Márton Weisz are also there at her house." Three were already home. From somewhere they turned up. They came home a couple of days before, also labor camp workers.

Mrs. Dudás wasn't a Jewish woman. Her son had converted to Judaism and had married Ernö Mandel's sister. That's why Ernö Mandel had gone to her house when he returned with Icus Wassermann, Gyula's older brother.

So we went there, the ones I came back with: Isaac Guttman, Joska Löwy, and Sanyi Frankel who was from Tarcal. Mrs. Dudás lived behind the Post Office. They were very nice and gave us something to eat. She said we should stay there for the night. Everyone had their blanket and we lay down on the floor and slept. We were used to this for years. In the morning she probably gave us something to eat and we went over to our houses.

And there was nothing, nothing, there was absolutely nothing. Nothing, nothing, nothing. In the garbage pile there was a lot of garbage and from that, the old photographs I could gather up. I only found those and some Jewish books that had also been thrown in the garbage. They had taken away the furniture, everything. I never found it.

The house was too damaged, so I couldn't move into it. The roof was in very bad shape, everything was. There wasn't a window on it and the door was completely broken. Not a piece of furniture was there, absolutely nothing. That had all been stolen. They took away everything. There was nothing.

The next day, an abandoned house that we found in good shape, a Jewish house, we cleaned out and in that we settled down. With the other two, Ernö Mandel and Icus Wassermann, all six of us moved into this house. It was Bernát Klein's house, a few houses away from Mrs. Dudás. No one had come back from the Bernát Klein family.

Fuchs house, 1991

Dad's father, Henrik Fuchs, had it built
when he married Dad's mother, Ida Billitzer, in 1891

Dad and Henry were both born in this house

There was a baker in Tokaj, Stajnovics. He had officially shortened his name to Stoján. He wasn't Jewish. He was Serbian and a very good man. He gave for free however much bread we needed. I later learned from your mother that he also had given them free baked goods when they were ghettoized on the Temple grounds before being deported.

József Stoján

Tokaj, circa 1930s

From yearbook of *Tokaji Ipartesület*
(Tokaj Merchants and Craftsmen Association)

Photo courtesy of Lajos Löwy

And then we went out of town and either we bought or we got potatoes and vegetables and we cooked for ourselves. Many men were there for a couple of days by then, and afterwards they went on their own.

The second day we were home, I went with Ernö Mandel to the bakery for the bread and a Russian soldier with a rifle grabs us. He grabs our arms and drags us to a place where there were two sacks of flour that needed to be taken down to the bakery. Well, we picked each one up, they were very heavy, we could hardly carry them, and we took them down to the bakery for him while he came behind us with the rifle. We put them down and then we could go on. They made bread for the Russian soldiers from that flour.

Everywhere in the city there were groups of Russian soldiers. In all the cities there were Russian soldiers. On the streets there was no one else at all. It was winter, there was a lot of snow, and no one was there but the Russian soldiers who were strolling.

Another day I was going again with Ernö Mandel and a Russian soldier grabs us again and takes us into a stable. There were about six horses there. The soldier presses this metal pitchfork into our hands that we should shovel the manure, and he instead is watching us with a rifle. Never in my life did I shovel manure! Oh, God! There I scraped ineptly and he started screaming at me, a word of which I didn't understand. So he threw down his rifle very angrily, took off his coat, came over, and takes the shovel away! And as he was showing me how to do it better, I snuck out. I was familiar with the area, went into the first side street, and ran all the way to the end and out.

In the afternoon my friend came home. He had worked there all day shoveling manure. If I stay there, it doesn't help. I should save myself and he himself, too. He said that he turned around and "where did you go?" And he said that the soldier ran out and came back with *another* man so that someone else would help him!

So then for a few days I cleaned up over at my house and started to repair it. The rest of the men did the same to their houses that they found in the same condition. Almost every day one or two more men came back and they couldn't move into any of their houses either because all their houses were in such bad shape. All the Jewish houses had been broken into or a bomb had reached them. The houses had been ransacked, the windows were broken, the doors torn up. When they arrived in the city, they were told they could go to Mrs. Dudás, and we went over to see them.

So, I was living with this little group for a while. A few days later there were about twelve of us. We saw that there were a few Jewish houses left with furniture that they couldn't carry away. So we decided that somehow we should board up the windows, the doors, and save the furniture, especially because some of it was very nice.

We decided to rent out that furniture so that if the Jewish owners come back, then their furniture would have been saved and could be returned to them. So we rented them out, not to Jews, but to the Christians, because they, too, had lost a lot during the war and they needed furniture. We had them sign a document that if anyone came back, their furniture would be returned to them. But no one came back and the furniture remained with the people who had rented them.

When we saw people in town, they would say, "So you escaped? How did you escape? Where were you?" Well, we didn't tell everything. I only said that I was in labor camp and we came back, here we are, we were liberated. And then they started to say, "Poor Mr. so and so, those poor people they took away. And how we tried to help, we took in food for them and we took this and that. I took bread in there for Mrs. so and so, I even baked *pogácsa* and took it in. And that nasty policeman, he didn't allow me to give it.

He chased us away, but the little I could, I took in. For the little children I would have taken a little milk, but the nasty policeman wouldn't let me. And when already early morning they took them away and I would have taken something in, well, they were no longer there. They took the poor things to the ghetto." All of them were good. And we listened. But what bad things they did, they didn't speak about that. Everyone was amazed to see us. "Oh, how happy I am that you came back!"

Then everything continued as before, as if nothing happened. For us it didn't matter either, we were busy, we had to live from doing something. We didn't concern ourselves with anything else.

And then we waited, everyday we waited, that perhaps tomorrow, somehow somebody from our family will come home, that we would hear about somebody. And then we realized that they are not coming home.

I asked about my family as soon as I came back, about my brother and my sisters. I heard nothing, nothing, absolutely nothing.

My sister Ilonka and her husband Samu Katz were married in 1926 in Nyiregyháza and then moved to Vásárosnamény where Samu was from and where their three children were born: Imre, we called him Imike, Márta, and Lacika. I later went there to see if anyone had come back. I heard that they had been deported to Auschwitz.

While I was there, a neighbor of theirs brought over Samu's silver watch. Samu had told her, "Give it to whomever in the family comes back if I don't." So she gave it to me. Some of their furniture was still in their house. I took it back to Tokaj to start our household with. This neighbor also said that there was a woman in the town who was the same age as Ilonka and who knew her before the war. She said that she was in the same *láger* with Ilonka. She said that Márta got sick first and died, then Ilonka got sick and died also.

When they were deported in 1944, Imike was 17, Márta was 15, and Lacika was 11. Ilonka was 44 and Samu was 52.

Initially Samu was in a labor camp for a while, but because he was older he was released. He was a big fellow. Sometime in '46, a man said he was with him in Auschwitz and that Samu never felt well. One day, Samu came back from work and just rolled over and died. I never heard anything about the two boys.

Dad's sister Ilonka, oldest son Imike, and husband Sámuel Katz

Vásárosnamény, circa 1930

Márta, Lacika (Lászlo), and Imike (Imre) Katz

children of Dad's sister Ilonka and husband Sámuel

1932

Imike (Imre) Katz

oldest son of Dad's sister Ilonka and Sámuel Katz

Bar Mitzvah, 1941, Vásárosnamény

Lacika, Márta, and Imike Katz

children of Dad's sister Ilonka and Sámuel Katz

circa 1940

My brother Vilmos was in the same labor camp as me until one day he had an accident working and had his first epileptic seizure. It was terrible, a terrible thing to see. So they sent him to a hospital and then back to Tokaj, and he never returned to the labor camp. It was still so early in the war.

He was later deported to Auschwitz with his wife Ella Glattstein and their two daughters, Noémi who was 9 years old and Judit who was 7. None of them survived. Vilmos was 43 years old. Ella was from Mezöcsár where they had gotten married, but they moved to Tokaj where the children were born.

Ella Glattstein and Dad's brother Vilmos Fuchs

Mezöcsár, 1930

Noémi and Juditka Fuchs

children of Dad's brother Vilmos and wife Ella Glattstein

Tokaj, circa 1940

My brother-in-law Sándor Friedlander went to labor camp in 1940. He never returned. Later I learned that my sister Márjem and their little boy Palika who was 6 years old were deported to Auschwitz and we never heard what happened to them. Not even a picture of Márjemka or of her husband remained, only of Palika.

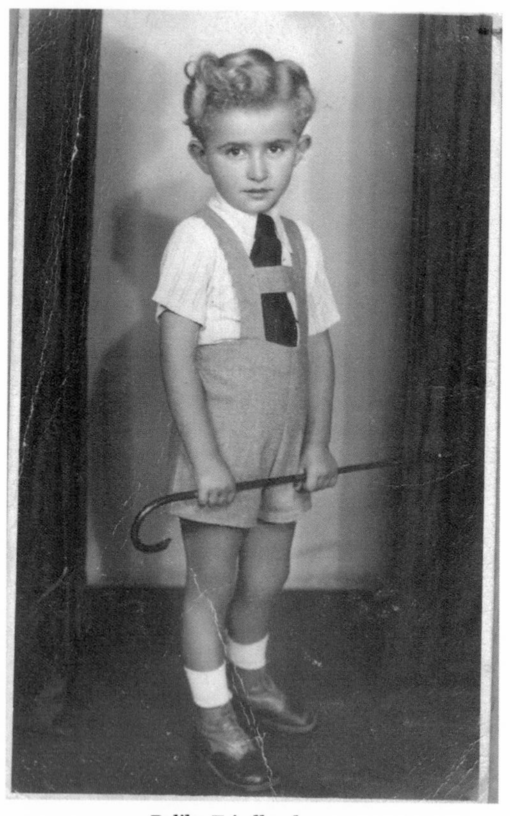

Palika Friedlander

son of Dad's sister Márjemka and husband Sándor Friedlander

Tiszalúc, circa 1942

Márjemka was dark blond, very beautiful, and resembled my mother. They were married in Tokaj in 1938 but lived in Tiszalúc. Sándor was in the meat business. In order to do something with his money, being afraid to put it in a bank during the war years, he offered that he would buy some cattle with me, fatten them up for a year, and sell them in Italy. Once he bought eight steers for me, but soon after I was taken to labor camp and never knew what happened to the cattle.

Once I was walking in town and recognized a jacket of mine on someone. "This is my jacket, where did you buy it?" "I got it here." "This is mine and I want it back." And he gave it back. And the pants of that same jacket I found on someone else. "Where did you buy it?" "I bought it here." Well, he, too, gave it back.

At some point, a friend of mine came home, Elus Frankel, Dezsö Frankel's son who was also a second cousin of mine. His grandmother – his mother's mother – and my grandfather – my father's father – were siblings. He came home sick and asked that I be with him until he gets well again. He had a cold and fever, everything. The pharmacist came up and gave him an injection and he got better. There wasn't a doctor at that time in town. So I was with him, looked after him, cooked for him. Then he says that I should stay with him until someone comes home, that I, too, am alone, he is also, we should stay together. Elus's wife and two small children didn't come back.

Another family, by the name of Szartori, had been living in the house during the war, an old woman with her daughter and son-in-law. She was a noblewoman from a Baron family. Elus let them continue to live there but he asked them to give him a part of the house. It was lucky that the family had been living there because all the furniture had therefore been saved. Before the war, Elus and his father Dezsö, a widower (his wife was Israel

Gross's daughter), had lived in that house with the whole family. Elus was one of six kids, three daughters and three sons. All of Dezsö's children had children of their own before the war. Dezsö was deported to Auschwitz as were all the children and their families. They were very rich, while we were middle class and therefore the poor relations. They were very nice to us but there was a certain distance.

While living there, I bought a bicycle. I would go out to towns, buy tobacco to make cigarettes, or I took out shoe polish that I had made and would sell them in little stores. One day, someone broke into the house and stole the bicycle. I managed without it after that.

I started making cigarettes because you couldn't get them at the time. A farmer brought in a bunch of tobacco for me, big leaves already dried, and I cut them up with a sharp knife into really small pieces. Someone made a little pipe from cigarette paper for me that I used to stuff the cigarettes with. I also made some boxes from old cardboard boxes and glued them together and stacked 100 cigarettes into a box. Day and night for about two weeks I cut the tobacco, made the cigarettes and the boxes. When I had about 100 to 200 of those boxes, I packed them into a big package like a backpack and took them up to Budapest where I sold them for a good profit.

Not long afterwards, a sister-in-law of Elus came home. She survived, a girl named Cipi. She might have been 18, 20 years old. How did this girl get here? She was from Yugoslavia and when they rounded everyone up there, she happened to be here visiting her older sister, Elus's wife, and she couldn't return. She ended up in the ghetto here, and then they took her from here but somehow she managed to escape and made it back. There was nowhere for her to go, so she stayed here with her brother-in-law. And he asked me then if I would stay and live here with them, too, because he didn't want to be alone with his sister-in-law.

A short time later, another girl came back from some camp. She was also a girl of about 18, 20 years old, a cousin of Elus, very nice. Anikó was her name and she also was a girl by herself. She was a very beautiful girl. She was blond. Cipi, on the other hand, had black hair.

So the two girls and Elus and I lived there. Elus also occupied himself with something. While I was busy making cigarettes he bought and sold wine, and we put the money together. The girls stayed home, cooked, washed, cleaned, and we ate and lived together.

Now then, Russian soldiers were always going through the city, marching somewhere. You see, the entire country was overrun with Russians. Budapest, as well as some other cities, was still under the Germans, and the Russian soldiers were proceeding forward. At night they lodged somewhere.

Well, they went to City Hall where they were told that here is a big house and they could lodge here. This was, indeed, a big house. There were about eight rooms and only a few were occupied.

So one night, someone from City Hall came and brought over four Russian soldiers, and that they are hungry. It turned out that one of them was Jewish and I spoke Yiddish with him. He explained that they are marching through here and that they were officers. There was anti-Semitism in Russia also, but they didn't deport the Jews there. The Jews served in the regular army, and in fact, they filled high officer positions.

So they are hungry. Well, what do we have? We gave them bread and butter, or margarine, and onions. And they needed wine. Well, we had wine, so we gave them wine also.

Now then, one of the soldiers became very drunk and says that he heard that two girls are here, two very beautiful girls. My friend happened not to be home just then, he was occupied with some business; so I was alone with the two girls.

When the soldiers rattled on the gate and we saw them, I sheltered the two girls in the last room. I told them they should stay there, lock the door and be quiet. I then said to the soldiers that there aren't any girls here. So then a big search went on, from room to room looking for them. They arrived where the girls were hiding and knocked on the door and of course, no reply. It was locked, so they yelled, "Open up!" I pleaded in Yiddish with that Jewish officer that he shouldn't allow this, "Here are two Jewish girls. Don't allow them to be hurt." He said that he cannot do anything.

The other soldier demanded to open the door because otherwise he will break it down. So I had to say to the girls, "He will break down the door. I'm sorry, open up." But I stood in front of the door as they opened it and one of the soldiers started to go in. I grabbed him and restrained him as I said to the girls, "Climb over, run to the other house! There are people there and run over there!" While I was wrestling with the drunken soldier the girls ran away and eventually I did, too. This was in the middle of the night around two o'clock.

Well, of course, I didn't want to leave the house. So I hid down in the yard in a corner. There in the stairway, shivering, I was so cold, I waited. The soldiers will go away in the morning, I thought. Finally, they came down. The Jewish soldier came in front and said in Yiddish that he thanks us for everything and that everything is in order. And the one who I grabbed and threw down came over to me and hit me in the chest so hard that I fell down. Well, he was angry because I saved the two girls.

Not long after, I took out the permit for a store. My father's store had been next door to our house. Down in the yard there was a long building that wasn't worth rebuilding. A stonemason said he would tear it down and build another one, where there was a woodshed and a summer kitchen, in exchange for the material that would be left over.

I started selling salt, sugar, paprika, pepper, whatever could be obtained. Shoe polish, shoelaces, soda bicarbonate, paints, whatever you could get. I went up to Budapest to buy what was available and brought them home and sold them.

Later on, people opened up stores everywhere in town. Miki Glück's father also came back and later opened up a store. He was already married before the war and his wife and two little girls didn't come back. Then this Ettuska came back and later they got married. I don't know whether she had children or not but her husband didn't come back.

It was not easy. We worked day and night. On Saturday we rested and I closed the store Friday afternoon. Once when I was doing that, some people came from the city needing birch brooms to clean the streets. I told them that on Saturday I don't open the store, please wait, that by 5 or 6 o'clock Saturday night *Shabbes* will be over and then they should come. I opened then and they bought 20-25 brooms and swept the streets at night so that it would all be ready for some parade that Sunday. So people respected that on Saturday I don't open the store.

Meanwhile, we sent packages to our Commanding Officer's wife and child. Some of the labor camp men knew that they were living in Budapest. We took turns sending basic food supplies, for life was hard for everyone after the war. These monthly packages went on for a year or more, and I remember each time it was my turn, she wrote a nice thank you note. With one of these she included a picture of him.

The Commanding Officer

Budapest, 1942

In response to the last package, she said not to send her any more because she had found a good job and now could provide on her own for herself and the child. At the same time, she wrote that she had received word from Russia. Her husband had died in a labor camp in Siberia. He was a young man, our Commanding Officer, only in his 40s. And he had saved our life.

9

Jewish life in Tokaj after the war

side of original benches in the Tokaj Synagogue

When we came back, the big Synagogue was already in pretty bad shape. The roof was still on but all the windows were broken. We found perhaps two or three Torahs and repaired them. I think someone might have put them away during the war and brought them back.

Before the war, there had been 25 to 30 Torahs. You see, it was an old congregation. From everywhere people bought Torahs or someone moved here and brought a Torah with him. At least 20 of them couldn't be used because they weren't kosher. I remember those Torahs were in such old faded covers and the Torahs so old that there were some people who sewed them together by hand. The ark was so big and so deep, like a walk-in closet. There were shelves placed on top of each other and on the side.

There was the *gabbai* and the *shammes* and two rabbis, a chief rabbi and an assistant rabbi. The head rabbi was Rabbi Akiba Strasszer. When he died, a couple years later it was Rabbi Nandor Jungreisz. They decided which Torahs we should use, which ones are the kosher ones. But on Simchas Torah, they took out every Torah for the procession in long lines. There were at least 200 people who took all the Torahs around seven times.

After the war, nothing was left of the Jewish community's records. Everywhere people moved in, they took everything, and most likely threw the documents in the trash or burned them. We found nothing.

First ten men came together. Then all of us came together and prayed in the Temple on Friday night and Saturday, and afterwards it was every morning. We went down to the Temple and prayed together.

My parents were very religious, honest people who fully believed without question in God, and I grew up in this belief. When I returned from labor camp, I was very depressed, especially since none of my family returned. I couldn't understand and I couldn't find an answer to why did all of this happen? Because of this, my faith in God was shaken, but I continued to be an observant Jew. I observed the Sabbath and holidays. I observed the dietary laws and ate only kosher food. I continued to live a traditional Jewish life.

Everyone resigned themselves to what had happened. What we believed was that the Good Lord had some purpose with this, that there *is* some purpose with this. And we believed and just waited and hoped that someone from our families would come home.

No one philosophized about any of this. Always our thinking was how could we make a living. We needed to buy clothes for ourselves, put our houses in order, and we needed to eat, of course. Religion we kept as it used to be.

We just spoke about the everyday happenings. There wasn't a radio to hear the news. In Tokaj we didn't know anyone who had a radio then. And it wasn't allowed to listen to foreign programs. That was forbidden by the Hungarian government and seriously punished. We didn't know anything. Occasionally, we got a newspaper from Budapest, but in the newspaper what they wrote was what was allowed for them to write. We didn't know anything at all.

In Tokaj someone started to write a newspaper. There was a printing shop and the newspaper was two pages. Once a week it appeared, but that, too, was only for a short time. No one bought it, so they stopped producing it.

And a Jewish newspaper could not possibly be. It was out of the question. Later, probably about a year later after Budapest was liberated, a Jewish paper was started there. The Jews organized themselves there. But in the countryside, we didn't see the Jewish newspapers.

10

Mom and her sisters come back

spools of thread from Mom's collection

Bözsi

Mom's older sister

It was in the middle of the night in August when we arrived to Tokaj. We had taken the train from Budapest to Keresztúr, a little town next to Tokaj, and from there we came in a car. We couldn't go to our own house because gypsies had moved into it. Miklós had already told us that in Budapest. He came back in January from labor camp. We stayed in Budapest for a while because when we got there after the camps, Jenö said we looked so bad. We should have a little human form first before we go home.

So, we were standing there on the street, having no place to sleep, when two boys appeared. One was our cousin Argyus Rosenberg, Munis' younger brother. Oh, what great happiness there was! Argyus said that a few of them were living in the abandoned Rogner house, no one had come back from the Rogner family, and we could stay in the storefront of the house though they hadn't fixed it up yet. We slept on the floor and the next day we got a hold of beds from somewhere.

By then there was a soup kitchen set up at the Temple, upstairs where the Jewish school was. Well, the Temple was ruined and the stairs in such broken down condition, but they put a stove in and you could cook up there. We went there and always helped to cook. Altogether about 80 Jews came back and everyone went there to eat in the beginning.

When we came back, some people said that more Jews came back than left. Well, how could more come back when there were 1200 Jews in Tokaj? Only 80 of us came back, more labor camp workers than those of us who were dragged away to Auschwitz.

Mom (Ilona, Ica)

The day after we got home, Miksa and everyone came over to see us, the boys who had already come home from labor camp. And I was very proud that the next day I was already cutting material with the scissors Berta *néni,* my fiancée's mother, had given me in Budapest. The Rogner house we were staying in was a two-room place and there was a storefront where we slept.

On the third day, we went to City Hall to get a license and I opened up a tailor salon, "Engel Ilona *Nöi Szabómester,*" Women's Master Tailor. And Lajcsi Lazarovits, this Jewish boy who was a police captain, with some others painted the sign nicely. So everyone knew I had my diploma and I had two students. One was the daughter of a woman who wanted that she learn to sew well. For six months she was an apprentice and brought two *mázsa búza*, 100 kilograms of wheat, from Rakamaz. Another brought a liter of milk every day. So by then we had flour and milk, and for one liter of oil I made a dress.

There was a communal kitchen, but because I was working I didn't use it. And everyone stayed with us who came to Tokaj. There was room on the floor for them to sleep. But our former teacher Henrich Lefkovics said that this wasn't proper.

We heard when we got back that our parents did not survive. But we wanted to see our furniture, our sewing machine, something. We found our house, and like the other Jewish homes, it had been totally ransacked. What was my grandfather's furniture we did find. Before he died, he told his children that the bedroom furniture should be for me.

One Sunday as people were going to Church, we saw a girl on the street wearing a dress I had made for Pityu. She says "hello" and I see she is wearing that dress. "Please, wait a minute, I would like to ask you something, " I say. "Don't be angry, but this is my sister's dress that I made for her," a pink taffeta, plaid, two piece dress. My father had brought the material from Kassa. "No, no, my mother bought this," she said. "She got the dress from this person or that person."

"I tell you what," I said, "if under the arms there is a gusset, then this is my younger sister's dress. If there isn't a gusset, then it's yours." And she came into our house and indeed the gusset was there. Well, I remember my own work! "Just go to church," I told her. I just wanted to know. If she has this, then she also has more things of ours. I don't remember whether she gave it back, but we got some official papers, like a search warrant, from Lajos Lazarovics so that we could go to this girl's parents' house to see if we find things that used to be ours.

As Bözsi, Pityu, and I went in, we saw on the bed a rug I had someone make for me from the remnants of materials I had made dresses from for other people. The design of this rug was a copy of the rugs called Torontáli which were woven in Hungary. No one else in Tokaj had this kind, so it was very distinctive and easily recognizable. When I said this was my rug, they gave it to us without a problem.

On the door was a table runner, a handmade Kalotaszegi, which this kind of embroidery is called, white embroidery on white material. It was cut in half and was on the door window.

11

Getting married

Ilona Engel and Miksa Fuchs, February 1946

Mom (Ilona, Ica)

I had promised myself that I would wait five years for my fiancée Bandi to return. That would be January 1st, 1946. Miklós asked me if it would be alright with me if he and Pityu go ahead and get married first. It was first love for both of them. Well, my parents did not come back to ask. So, I said sure, and on September 24th on Pityu's birthday they had an engagement party and on November 22nd they got married.

Miksa and I knew each other a long time. At Pityu's wedding we went for a walk and he asked me to marry him. And I said to him, "My dear Miksa, don't be angry, but I want to wait until January 1st. But I won't marry anyone else but you."

Bandi and I would have gotten married in 1941, May 21st or June 21st, but they called him up in February for labor camp. It was such a sad thing when we had to say goodbye. First they were in Hatvan but I didn't go see him. On my birthday, March 31st, I got a package from him, a beautiful patent leather bag with daisies on it. He wrote and sent it from Budapest. He wrote every day from there but said that he can't say goodbye again, that I shouldn't go see him. Once I sent him a photograph with my hair up. He wrote back saying, "I don't like it like this. I like it better the way you usually wear your hair." It was the last letter I got from him.

Before we were deported I got a telegram. His mother in Budapest had received it and sent it to me. It said that Andor Goldstein had disappeared in Sztradyoszkol. That was in Russia, in a labor camp. Well, if someone died, they don't write that he died. Apparently, the entire squadron disappeared. This was sometime in 1942. But I just didn't want to give up hope, so I waited.

After Miksa asked for my hand, he told Elus Frankel he was living with that Ica said that if she waits until January 1st and Bandi doesn't come back by then, she will marry him. And Elus teased him, which wasn't nice of him, saying, "Well then, how do you feel that if there isn't a horse, an ass is good, too?" It wasn't nice but Miksa didn't take offense. He understood. He was really a very honorable man. He was a handsome man, a notable man, he was somebody.

And January 1st came and we were together, Miksa and I, with Elus and Cipi who I was good friends with. We were playing cards and talking. Suddenly at midnight, Elus broke a dish at the threshold to mark our engagement. We woke up Bözsi who was at home. Later she went up to Budapest with oil or sugar, supplies like this that were given to us for our work, and on Teleki Square she exchanged them for sheets and pillowcases and tablecloths, things that we needed.

We sent a telegram to Renée and Margit in America that I got engaged. And when I got a telegram back from them, everyone knew since Tokaj is such a small place. "In the interest of bringing you out, wait. Don't get married!" Miksa was out of town, in Miskolc or someplace, and I didn't even wait for him to come home. I telegrammed back because the response had been prepaid: "My groom's name is Miksa Fuchs. He was born in 1911, June 30th. Prepare the documents like this!" And then Margit wrote, since she had gone to school with Miksa, and so they knew that I wouldn't get married to just anyone, "If you have gotten married already, just don't have children!"

So then on February 12, 1946 we got married. And they cleaned the house before the wedding for a liter of oil.

Dad (Miksa)

We set up the *chuppah* at the abandoned Jewish house Ilona and her sisters were living in. It was on a Tuesday, February 12th, and Margit and Klári Blitz came from Sárospatak. Herman Davidovics, who for a long time was a cantor and rabbi and came back from deportation, joined the couples together then. Rabbi Jungreisz had perished with his wife and child.

We bought some fish, and Bözsi and Ilona cooked it. Everyone, friends, cooked and baked. The table was set and there was a big feast for dinner with about 60 people, our Jewish and non-Jewish friends as well.

At the wedding celebration there were a lot more people, I don't even know how many, 100 maybe, because it turned out to be a noteworthy day. Not since anyone could remember had it ever happened that the Bodrog flowed back stream! The Bodrog flows into the Tisza River by the bridge. It was such cold times that both rivers froze over. When the ice melted, and the water pushed up the ice, the ice traveled down, and at the bridge the ice piled up all together. The water couldn't go down because the ice had accumulated so much and kept the water up so high that the river flowed backwards. No one could go across the bridge that was also damaged.

So all the people who had come over to Tokaj to the *piac*, the open market, couldn't go home. And here we have the wedding celebration, so everyone came in. There were gypsies playing music and everyone danced. After midnight the guests left. We also left and went to bed. The wedding was over, you can kiss the bride, and life resumed.

Someone had given me ten dollars as a wedding present. Ten American dollars was a lot of money, and for that I bought so much merchandise in Budapest that I had it in four sacks and sent them home on the train as personal luggage. I remember a porter at the train station brought them out. I arrived home but the four sacks of goods didn't. "It will come tomorrow," they said. Not tomorrow, nor the next day. They never arrived.

I made a claim,and a document came back saying that the Russians broke into this and that train, and they took everything. Who really stole it all you don't know. Well, there weren't laws then and I was naïve that I sent it. I thought it would arrive and it didn't come. Someone had stolen it, anyone, a railway employee. No one looked for it. So there I was without a *fillér*, a penny. So I started again from scratch. It was like this not only with me. This kind of thing happened to many people.

12

Life in Tokaj, 1948-1956

Mom, Dad, and Henry
Tokaj, 1949

The first Jewish child born in Tokaj after the war was Lenke Klein's son Lacika. Henry was the second in 1948. Gabi Glück was the third. Then I don't know who else. Then you, Márta, came along in 1950.

We sold a lot of different goods in our store, including candles that we made. The Catholics and probably the Christians, too, celebrated the religious memorial day for the dead on November 30th. The custom was that they went out to the cemetery and put candles on the gravesite, lit them, and prayed.

Because you couldn't get candles then, I bought some wax. It was hard to get that, too. I went everywhere for it. Even in Budapest you couldn't get it easily because people needed candles everywhere since in many places there was no electricity. I melted the wax and poured it into *minyon* paper, the kind they put little pastries in. On the bottom we put little wicks. Henry must have been about two years old, and he placed the candles into boxes.

Nowhere else could you get these candles, only in our store. "Oh, may God bless Fuchs *Úr*!" people would say. They liked them so much that already early morning they stood in front of the store waiting for them. All night Ilona and I worked making these candles, and by 6 o'clock in the morning at least 50 people were there waiting for them. "For me, please, for me!" And for everyone we sold a box that had 10 candles in it.

Once when Henry was in the store, he was helping himself to the chocolate wafers he loved so much. I hadn't noticed that he was eating them until a customer came in and asked for some. "Certainly, " I said, and went to the bin to serve her. Much to my surprise, there were only a few left!

When the Communists came to power, I didn't think they would take the store away since it was such a small store. In the mail one day at home, I got an official letter stating that I must close the store as soon as I receive the letter, and take the key down to City Hall.

I hadn't even finished reading the letter when an official came in with a copy of it and told me to get my coat and go with him to my store. I gave him the key, he locked the door, and I went back home while he went to City Hall. In a few days, they said they would do the inventory.

I was there for it. It was done in a few hours. A month later, I got a portion of the money, and a few months after that, I got the second and final payment, all of which Ilona used to buy a knitting machine.

I only got 25% of what the entire stock was worth. “Take it or leave it,” they said to me. I couldn’t do anything about it. It didn’t even occur to me that they would not be fair about it.

Dad's grocery store, bottom right corner

Tokaj, circa 1948
historic postcard

(discovered on Facebook, 2011)

Marta

Henry and I, of course, remember our small grocery store that was a few doors down and across the street from where we lived on the main road in town. We used to play there, and after school we often went to get money from Dad in order to go to the *cukrázda*, the ice cream store on the opposite corner.

The building where the store was is now the town's museum, featured on postcards over the years. When Henry and I went back to Tokaj in 1990, we went to the museum with the Mayor who gave us a personal tour. When we returned later to ask if there were any museum brochures, along with some leaflets we were given a calendar which the local printer had designed, featuring reproductions of paintings by a Tokaj amateur painter, Samuel Helm.

As we flipped through the pages, admiring the beautiful Monet-like watercolors for each month, we came to October and nearly fainted. There on that page, in 1990, was the painting Samuel Helm had done of Dad's store back in 1948.

On subsequent trips, we visited Samu *bácsi* and his lovely wife, Lili *néni.* He showed us literally hundreds of his 8" x 12" watercolors, including Dad's store, gathered together in hand stitched notebooks. Lili *néni* made needlepoint pillows of many of his paintings, and these were gracing the couches and chairs in their home.

A few years later on January 20th, Samu *bácsi* passed away at age 98. A year or so later when Henry was in Tokaj again he went to see Lili *néni*, and there was a package waiting for him. "Samu *bácsi* wanted you to have this." It was the painting of Dad's store.

Fuchs Miksa
FUSZER és VEGYES

On the trip with Dad and Henry in 1991, we went back to the museum. As I was standing in one of the rooms mesmerized by the frescoes, Dad walked in. “Aren’t these incredibly gorgeous?” “Oh yes, I remember playing here when I was a child. The house belonged to a rich relative.” Henry and I had no idea.

It would be years later we would learn that it was this very house, the big Dezsö Frankel house, that Dad lived in with Elus Frankel when they came back from labor camp and where Dad nursed Elus back to health. It was the house where Dad rescued the two young girls from the drunken Russian soldier. And it was in this house that Mom and Dad were officially engaged on New Year’s eve 1946 when Elus brought out a dish and broke it at the threshold.

Dad

The *mozi,* the movie theater, was down the street from where we lived. We always went to the movies, at least twice a week. It was very inexpensive and we even took you and Henry. And Henry would always say, "I have to pee" right at the most exciting point! At the best part I had to take him out to pee! And "*Apuka,* I am thirsty." Well, because we always took some water in a bottle, we didn't have to leave to get a drink, but he always had to pee!

I remember once when we went with you two to a movie, there was a scene with SS soldiers wearing a big swastika in an office, and they were interrogating a woman, a Jewish woman with a young boy. And then one of the SS with the big swastika slapped her in the face and the woman fell down and the little child began to cry from fright. To this, *Anyuka* and I stood up, took you two children, and left. I don't know what the film was but we just couldn't watch it. No one came out, only us. It was probably a propaganda film, the Russians against the Germans, showing that the Germans had done this. We had lived this kind of thing, so why see it?

Mainly there were Russian films that were comical and we laughed so much at them. Men with big fat stomachs were drinking and having a good time and were fighting with the women.

Tokaj, 1951

Hajduszoboszló, 1952

in our backyard, Tokaj, 1955

Henry

In school, I recall being told that Lenin was writing to his niece and nephew, promising that he would come for Christmas, and some difficulty arose. The children still believed, though, and he actually made it and brought them presents. These stories about Lenin were like the ones about Abe Lincoln that I heard in America when I was in 3rd or 4th grade.

One day, the teacher asked us boys to stay after school. In the classroom there were chairs in front with rectangular writing surfaces. Someone new came in, a young woman, high school age, good looking, friendly, wearing a red kerchief, like a bandana, around her neck. She sat down on the table of one of the chairs, which was something distinctly different than anyone else had done.

She told us that we would be doing great things together, like young executives, and that we were all going to get red kerchiefs. I don't remember doing anything together. It might have been the Fall of '56 when we soon left in December. I remember she was friendly and chatting with us. This was probably the first step to the Young Communists League.

In the middle of the conversation, she asked how things were in class, "And which one of you is the best student?" Two things struck me about this: one, that I had never heard that question before, and two, that a bunch of the kids pointed to me. It was the first time I remember having any sense of academic achievement.

13

Escaping, 1956

family photo, circa 1950s

Marta

One evening after dinner, we are listening to the old wooden radio mounted on the wall. It is our nightly ritual to tune in. It wasn't actually a real radio like Sárika *néni* and Miklós *bácsi* had next door which broadcast directly. Instead, we got a few programs piped in via the Post Office down the street. At 8 o'clock each night, we heard the familiar voice of the radioman call out to us, "Children, are you in bed yet?" "NO!" Henry and I would yell back, laughing hysterically. We'd still be eating or just starting to get our pajamas on.

So on this night in late October 1956, we are listening to our cousin Robi playing the viola. A concert by his string quartet is being broadcast from Budapest.

As we're enjoying the music, suddenly we hear a lot of commotion, the program goes off the air, and the radio goes dead. We later learn that the Revolution had broken out in Budapest that day, October 23rd, and the radio station had been taken over by the Freedom Fighters.

Many weeks later, on a Friday night in early December, I wake up to see all the lights on and Mom and Dad scurrying about. They are taking things out of drawers and cupboards in the big room we all sleep in. It feels exciting, bright lights and activity in the middle of the night. I can't sleep, so I amuse myself by playing a game. I sit up with my down cover on my back, wait a few seconds, and crash down on the cool sheets. Up and down I go repeatedly. Mom tells me to try to sleep but I am wide awake. It's fun to play and be up with Mom and Dad. Little do I know at six and a half playing my game, that they are getting ready for us to leave Hungary and soon we'll be escaping into the night for another world.

When it's time to go, all of us dressed, and I'm holding Henry's half-size violin wrapped in paper with a string around it, I march directly to the chest in the kitchen to get my favorite red and white polka dot ball Bözsi *néni* had given me. But it's not there. It's always there, I'm thinking. Where could it be? Mom says we have to leave, and so I do, glancing back at the chest, wondering, as we go out.

After traveling all night, we are standing in the middle of a train station in Budapest. I feel chaos all around me. People with suitcases and bundles are hurrying about, and somehow it feels that things aren't quite right, some tracks look broken, and trains aren't coming. Our relatives who live in Budapest are saying goodbye to us, and everyone is hugging and kissing and being very emotional. I don't know that it will be two decades before we see them again.

It's pitch black and freezing cold, and the snow is slushy

and slippery as we walk silently for hours across the border. We follow each other in a row behind our guide, a man I never saw before. He told us kids not to say a word, and if we have to pee, we should motion to someone and then we'll stop. It feels a bit bulky wearing several layers of clothing so that we don't have to carry them. Our outer layer is dressy because when we left home, Mom said we have to look dressed up so that if anyone stops us and asks, we are going to Éva and Robi's wedding. I'm not told that if we get caught, no excuse would work and we'd either be shot or sent back and thrown in jail.

After walking for hours, suddenly in a clearing over a bridge some people appear, big smiles on their faces, and they are coming toward us with open arms. Everyone with us bursts out talking, breaking hours of silence. Their excitement pierces the blackness and freezing air. People fall to their knees and kiss the ground, and before I know it delicious chocolate is melting warmly in my mouth.

We are taken into this big room with bales of hay all over the place for us to sleep on. Mom glances down and shakes her head, "Bözsi *néni* is not going to like this." For some reason, Bözsi *néni* and Miki *bácsi* didn't come with us and they weren't here yet. But there were tons and tons of other people already here.

The next day, they take us in buses to a refugee camp, and then to several others as months go by. Somewhere I find myself playing an old upright piano and everyone is enjoying it. Some people tell me how sweet and talented I am. Somewhere I am sitting on top of a bunk bed in the middle of a gigantic room filled with people everywhere I look. It is noisy and chaotic as I look around in disbelief. I have never seen so many people in one room before. They are all in little groups, grown-ups and children, and everyone is always talking and busy doing things. I just keep watching, totally amazed.

Then something scary happens. We have just gotten on a bus and I am sitting near the back, next to the window on my right. As I look out, I am surprised to see that Miklós *bácsi* is arguing with some man. As they're yelling at each other, they start fighting and shoving. The next thing I know, Dad jumps out of his seat, rushes down the aisle, and breaks up the fight.

Later that day or the next, we are on a train and I'm watching Dad and Miklós *bácsi* who are sitting opposite each other. Neither of them is saying a word. They are not even looking at each other. Both of them have a serious look on their face. Are they mad at each other? When are they going to talk to each other again?

Years later I learn that the fight outside the bus was just one of many anti-Semitic incidents that occurred along the way. "And everyone was sick and tired of it all," Mom explained.

Henry

In the refugee camp in Salzburg, four of us were in two bunk beds, and there were hanging dividers between us for privacy. They were these makeshift curtains or blankets hung on a string. We had this little room with two bunk beds on each side with just enough space to get up in between. I remember playing there on the floor with the Trix metal pieces some people got me for my birthday. They were like Erector sets kids have now. I still have them.

At another refugee camp, in one of the cottages, I remember hiding under a table with others, adults and kids, after some of the adults had barricaded the door. Lots of men were shouting outside and banging on the door, trying to break it down, while inside the Jews were cowering under the tables.

Dad and I, with another man, went into town to report this situation to one of the Jewish agencies helping refugees. The next morning, buses arrived to transfer all of us Jewish Hungarians to another camp. That's how we ended up in that beautiful place Badkreutzen.

Marta

In Badkreutzen, Henry, Dad, and I are having so much fun sleigh riding. Miki *bácsi* made us a sled from some scraps of wood. Down the hill we go, cracking up whenever we tip over. The sun is sparkling and the snow is glittering.

On the ship coming to America, I wish I wasn't always seasick. I hate feeling so nauseated all the time. After throwing up I actually feel better, but then all the swaying continues, up and down and side to side, making me sick all over again. I'm always thirsty and want to drink some water, but for some reason we aren't supposed to drink from the tap. One night as I'm brushing my teeth, I tell Mom how thirsty I am. She says I can take a little sip and it feels better, though I wonder if I'll be sick from the water now.

I miss being with Dad and Henry. They are with the men on the other side of the ship and we can only visit them at certain times. One day, Henry and I are sitting on his bed opening our navy blue cloth bags we got from the Red Cross. Inside are all these treasures, tiny little soaps and toothpaste and little toys, and we are all excited showing them to each other. The bag is so soft, and I love the deep blue color of it. And it's fun to pull it closed with the drawstring on top.

Henry

I remember going to services with Dad on the ship. This was for me another adventure. We went into this small room about 15 square feet, and it was packed with people, men only, and they were praying. There were folding chairs set up around the perimeter. It must have been the first or second day of our voyage because I was really feeling queasy and I only felt that bad in the beginning. Dad asked me, "Will you be okay for a while sitting here?" because he wanted to do the *Amidah*, the silent prayer, standing with the other men.

You and Mom were in a smaller room than Dad and I were. We had hammocks with a couple dozen men in a big room. You had bunk beds in a smaller room with just a few families.

I still have the Red Cross bag that we got and took it once to Sam's class. The teacher asked me to speak about coming to America for their study of immigration in connection with Thanksgiving.

Marta

We have regular emergency evacuation drills. We all have to put on these balloon-like orange vests I can hardly move in since they're so big and poufy, and follow each other in lines to various parts of the ship. We keep practicing this drill but luckily nothing bad ever happens. They tell us we need to do this in case something does happen.

Eating in the cafeteria is fun. There's always this strange

stuff that's bright red and cut in squares. It's sticky and really sweet and keeps wiggling as I stare at it on my plate. Then there's this pink fruit that's bigger than an orange. It's cut in half and tastes really bitter and squirts all over the place. We all sprinkle sugar on it, but even then it tastes bitter. They also give us something to drink made out of tomatoes. Again we all pour sugar into it to make it taste better.

It is really fun to sit up on deck in the cool ocean air with everyone, talking and playing. Dad tries to teach me to count to ten in English. I say the numbers as I count on my fingers behind my back but somehow I always end up saying "ten" when I still have one finger left over! We all laugh and I try again.

Finally, one day we suddenly start seeing tall buildings through the ocean fog, and people are pointing excitedly to a huge statue in the water, the Statue of Liberty. Many people fall to their knees and kiss the floor of the ship. Henry remembers that people burst out singing the Hungarian National Anthem, "probably because it was the only song everyone knew." We have finally arrived to America after 10 days and nights of being seasick. We pull into the harbor, and early the following morning stand in line forever, waiting to get off. It is February 15, 1957.

Relatives greet us and everyone is hugging and crying with such happiness. We are put on a bus and taken to another camp, Camp Kilmer in New Jersey. Everything seems the same as in previous camps, with hundreds of people all around. But I don't understand why people are arguing and fighting, shoving and wrestling with each other. Here we are in America, what's the problem now?

Two decades later I found out. My piano teacher's husband, Felix Polk, was a student in social work in 1957 at Albert Einstein University in New York, and was one of the people working at Camp Kilmer. He was hired by HIAS, the Hebrew Immigrant Aid Society, to interview and process the Hungarian refugees because he spoke German and understood Yiddish.

"They were anti-Semitic incidents," he told me. "It was notorious. Some Nazi types had gone out, left Hungary. I remember talking to many refugees who told stories about anti-Semitism there at Camp Kilmer and also before. It was gross anti-Semitism, it was rampant, and there was some violence. We tried to take action. I reported the stories as I interviewed people. I think attempts were then made to isolate the Nazis coming in."

I couldn't believe it. All these Hungarians had managed to escape and make it safely to America, but the war was still not over more than a decade later. It was now continuing on different soil, the "land of the free" they had all risked their lives to reach.

Dad

When Henry was born in 1948 we applied for a passport and actually got it and Henry was on it. But we couldn't get a visa. We thought of going to America then because it would be a better life, a better world, and that there were no close relatives left here. As you know, your mother's two older sisters were already in America, so we wanted to be with them. So we waited, hoping that perhaps sometime we will be successful in obtaining a visa.

When the Revolution broke out in October of '56, many people were killed in Budapest and in some of the other large cities. The situation was very dangerous and unstable. Since the borders were not always guarded so well, many people tried to escape. Many of them were successful, but some were killed and some were caught and thrown in jail. There was also a lot of anti-Semitism and we didn't feel safe.

Tibi Kálmánovics came home to Tokaj and said, "If you want to go, I can help you," because he was not far from the border in Tatabány. He was the manager of a wholesale company, and every week trucks went to sell in that area. "And a truck would take you all the way to the border."

So I went up to Budapest, this was the end of November, and discussed it with Miki *bácsi* and Bözsi *néni* and they said yes, they want to leave, too, and come with us. The next day we went down to Tata and talked with Tibi. At home we already had discussed it with the Kohns (Sárika *néni* and Miklós *bácsi)* that I would arrange it. And Tibi said, "Monday early morning a truck goes here on the edge of the border. Be here the latest Saturday night." This was Wednesday.

I came home right away, it was Thursday night, and I told your mother. We packed immediately, and on Friday night, a dark, cold, and windy night, we left Tokaj. We locked the house and left everything there. It was 12:30 just after midnight and with the Kohns we took a carriage to the Keresztúr train station. We didn't dare leave from the Tokaj station because it would have been conspicuous since everyone knew us. Because this was not legal, if the police came, they would have prevented us, and they would have jailed us.

Immediately there was a connection to Tatabány and hours later we arrived there. Our contact placed everyone with somebody, with their friends, each family separately. We were told we shouldn't go out in the street, that we shouldn't be conspicuous that there are strangers here, "and at 6 o'clock in the morning you should be ready because the truck will be here for you."

This place we were put up in Tatabány was with a Jewish family and there was a woman with her little daughter. The woman said to us, "I cannot go because my son and my husband are sick, but here is my daughter." She was a 17-year-old young girl, Éva. "Take her with you. I want that at least *she* escape. And here is my sister's address and telephone number in Vienna. Call her up and she will know." We agreed and the young girl came with us.

The truck arrived at 6 o'clock in the morning and we went to get Bözsi *néni* and Miki *bácsi*, then picked up the Kohns, then straight out on the highway to the border. We arrived to the border in the afternoon, already it was getting dark earlier, and the chauffeur said, "Do you see that little light over there? That is a house. Go over there and they will help you." We walked perhaps an hour until we reached that house. It was cold, there was a lot of snow.

There were already 8 to 10 people with children also waiting at this house to be taken across the border. The old woman was very nice and immediately went out to milk the cow, then boiled the milk and gave some to you children and to everyone who wanted it. She said that her son will be here right away and he will make the arrangements.

Not much later her son arrived, a big man, and he said, "We can leave only at 12 o'clock midnight," or maybe 11, I no longer remember, "when the guards at the border aren't watching so carefully anymore." He was familiar with the border because every night he took people across.

The time of departure arrived. He came into the kitchen where we were waiting, since it was the warmest room in the small farmhouse, and said, "We can leave now." We were about 20 people. "No one should talk, there should be complete silence," and he gave some sedative to the babies. "Do you see over there the platforms? There the Russian guards are guarding the border. You have to go down here into a big ditch. There isn't any water in it, only snow, a lot of snow. You should walk there so that the guards shouldn't notice you."

We walked in a row in the dark, cold night for about 2 to 3 hours, in the deep snow in the ditches of the open fields in order not to be discovered. The man watched us and waved, "Come, come, come" as he was watching the guards.

All of a sudden, the guide stopped us and pointed to a

bridge far off in the distance. "Do you see the bridge over there?" You have to reach that bridge and then you are saved. Go across it quickly and you will find yourselves in Austria. I wish you lots of luck, God bless all of you!" and disappeared.

Well, we looked at each other in shock. We weren't sure what to do next. We hadn't expected the guide to just suddenly leave us. We started to walk toward the bridge very cautiously. It was hard to see in the dark night. It was a long walk until we reached it. We were lucky that it was not being guarded and we wondered why not.

As we crossed the bridge, we saw on the other side young people wearing green hats waiting for us. In German they greeted us, "Welcome, welcome!" They were really happy and hugged us and told us we were in Nicklesburg and that they are Austrian college students, volunteers who came out every evening to help the Hungarian refugees who came across.

They led us to a school building not too far away where there were 5 or 6 big rooms, every one of them packed with Hungarians who had been coming across there for days. In one of the rooms there was a table filled with different kinds of food and drink, bread, butter, cheese, oranges, everything. Everyone was tired. To those who were sleepy, "Here is the hay, lie down, pull on the covers," there were already blankets there, "and go to sleep." They said that in the morning a bus will come and take everyone to Linz, a big city in Austria.

In the morning the bus came and took us into Linz, and our group was taken to a big warehouse. Everyone tried to settle down there. There were only a few Jews among us and it was very anti-Semitic there. People were saying the Jews this and the Jews that. We felt very bad.

Since we had this young girl Éva with us, when we arrived there I went to inquire where the Jewish office, the

Joint, was. I took the young girl and Henry with me everywhere. Henry as you know was 8, almost 9 years old then. They both behaved themselves very well. I said that here is this young girl, what the situation is, and here is the telephone number of her aunt, she must be called. "I'll get the director." Right away they called this number and the aunt answered and yes, at this certain time the train comes here to Vienna. "Take her to the station and we will be waiting for her in Vienna." The Joint people had to leave shortly, so they gave the money to me so that I could purchase the ticket for the young girl.

So Henry and I went out to the train station with her. At that time in Austria it was the custom that the streetcar was free for the refugees, you didn't have to pay for the ticket. So we went out by streetcar to the train station. The train arrives and someone leans out the window, "Hey, Miska, Miska!" I look over there and recognize an old friend of mine who I was with in labor camp. "So what are you doing here?" he asks me. I tell him briefly, "Here is this young girl, her aunt is waiting for her in Vienna. Could you watch out for her?" "Oh, gladly!" And the next day we called her mother and her aunt. The young girl arrived safely.

We then went back to the Jewish office. Many of us Jews went and spoke with the director that here this situation is very dangerous for us Jews. They are being anti-Semitic and they should do something about it. He says in German, "Tomorrow morning at 9 o'clock, every Jewish person should be ready and we will send buses and we will take you to a very good place." So we went back and figured out who the Jews were and told them about this, and that they should be ready by 9 o'clock for the buses.

Exactly at 9 o'clock, 3 or 4 or 5 buses arrived. All the Jews got on and they took us to a beautiful place, Badkreutzen. It was a vacation place for the Swedish queen. There were these little cottages ion which they settled everyone, every family in a room. We felt very good there, we walked down to the village, we became acquainted with some very nice people, your mother helped them cut out some dress and iron it, and so everything was very nice. We were there for 3 or 4 weeks and we were taken care of by the American Joint, the United Jewish Welfare, and the Red Cross.

After about a month, they took us to Salzburg where we also were for about 2 or 3 weeks, but again they were very anti-Semitic there. Once, a bus arrived with Jews and these scoundrels surrounded it. They were the Arrow Cross, the Hungarian Nazis, saying, "Did you bring a lot of dollars, a lot of gold with you? Because the Jews are stuffed with tobacco, gold, and dollars." It was very, very unpleasant.

Meanwhile, from Salzburg we applied to America. To get the visa you needed sponsorship, which we got from Renée *néni* and Margit *néni*, that they will take responsibility for us. People who got this were put on the list and taken to Bremerhaven in Germany by train, and there immediately we were put on the ship where we waited for perhaps not even a day until the ship departed. The ship's name was General Walker, an American military transport ship. There were perhaps 600 Hungarian refugees on board. We slept in those hammocks, don't you remember? It was fine, comfortable. The ocean was very rough and many people got seasick, like your mother and you, poor things. Then 9 days later we arrived in America.

There were hordes of people in the harbor. Everyone was waiting because they inquired when the ship was going to arrive. And we spotted Renée *néni* there somewhere and we waived and ran to each other, embraced each other. We were then directed to go with a group that was being taken by bus to Camp Kilmer in New Jersey. Then Renée *néni,* Willy *bácsi,* and Allen came out from New York on Sunday to see us. Also the relatives from New Jersey, the cousins all came out.

We arrived to America on Thursday, February 15th. On Friday I remember they gave us a bottle of kosher wine for every family so that we could make *Kiddush.* We didn't do anything there, only register ourselves and stand in line for our food. The entire day was taken up by this. There was anti-Semitism there, too. Well, there weren't only Jews there.

I was sick and tired of it all, I would have wanted to get out of that camp, I would have wanted to settle down somewhere, I would have wanted to work somewhere, make a living I wanted to already. I was sick and tired of this. I just wanted to go out already from this great horde of people.

14

Reflections

Tisza River, Tokaj, 2011

On the trip back to Hungary with Henry and Dad in 1991, we were getting ready for bed one night in a small hotel in Czechoslovakia when Dad started chuckling:

"I remember the first time I slept in a real bed again after five years in labor camp. I just couldn't remember and tried to recall how I would get into it, whether I used to put my right foot in first or my left foot, and how I would swing in and lie down."

As he laughed, I tried to join in the humor of it, but it was the deprivation he experienced that I couldn't help focusing on. Getting into bed is something so automatic, yet it was no longer the case for him after the war. I admire him for being able to think about it with amusement, but for me it's infused with sadness and anger for what he had to endure.

"In labor camp we slept on the floor, sometimes on hay we would find, with a small blanket and our coat on top of that. Those who had brought it with them had a small pillow. Others rolled up their pants and used that for a pillow."

*

We're sitting in a Budapest restaurant, waiting for dinner. It was October 23, 1991, the 35th Anniversary of the Hungarian Revolution. Many shops were closed, and certain streets were blocked off. The newspapers warned it was forbidden to congregate in groups without a permit. All day I was thinking about why we left Hungary.

At the table next to us, a large group of German tourists were having a great time, talking, drinking, and laughing. I turned to Henry, "Do you have any feelings when you hear German spoken?" "Yes, I feel uncomfortable. But for me it's more the land that makes me feel uncomfortable." "Yes," I agreed, "it's the opposite of sacred territory." I recalled that years before, Henry had been invited to speak at a conference in Germany and we talked about his deep ambivalence about going. He decided to decline.

"You know, " Henry continued, "Picasso never returned to Spain and Horowitz couldn't go back to the Soviet Union for years. And I think about Spencer Tracy's response in 'Judgment at Nuremberg.' A German widow of an army general said to him, 'Not all of us are bad. We had no idea this was going on.' 'Yes, as far as I can determine,' he responded, 'there's not a single person in Germany who knew anything about this.'"

I turned to Dad and asked him if he had any feelings hearing German.

"No, why should I? You can't blame an entire people for what happened. I want to be for peace."

In 1994 Henry went to Germany after all, and Mom joined him. She later told me that a young German woman serving as her translator who knew about Mom's Holocaust history asked her, "How is it for you to be in Germany? Do you blame us for what happened?"

"And this is what I told her: 'How can I blame you? You weren't even born then yet.'"

*

"Do you think much about the Holocaust?" I asked Dad years later.

"Yes, when I wake up in the middle of the night, I often calculate how old my sisters and my brother would be had they survived. Some of them probably would be dead by now had they lived."

*

I'm walking with a friend on a sunny Spring day. Everywhere we turn, flowers are bursting forth in all their glory and we frequently stop to literally smell the roses.

As we pass by a charming little house, in the front window I notice beautiful embroidered curtains, white, parted in the middle, elegantly swept to each side. “Those curtains look like they might have been a tablecloth once,” I remark casually.

Suddenly and unexpectedly, I am no longer seeing those curtains, but looking at the image of the embroidered tablecloth I never saw that my mother’s mother once made. The one Mom told me she found hanging as curtains, cut in two, on a stranger’s kitchen window when she returned home from Auschwitz where her parents and most of her world remained.

I can never say "my grandmother," only "my mother’s mother." There is no relationship with her that I can claim as my own, only sorrow that I feel for my mother’s loss of her mother, and a vague inkling of possibility for me when I see my parents lovingly playing with my children.

*

Two weeks before Christmas and Chanukah when Jacob was in Kindergarten, I picked him up early from his afterschool program and we went to get his favorite treat at our local bakery. An unusually windy day prevented us from sitting outside, so we got back in the car to eat his chocolate chip cookie and drink his carton of milk. As we ate and talked, we watched the lady in the bakery begin to paint holiday decorations on the storefront windows. She dipped a sponge into green paint, and with a stencil of a Christmas tree, created a textured replica on the glass.

Just as we began to put on our seatbelts and head home, we saw her dip another sponge into yellow paint, and with a different stencil begin to fashion a Star of David in bright, glowing, vivid yellow, the same color and diameter as the yellow stars during the war.

My heart stopped, then pounded with heightened awareness for the past and in protection of the present sitting next to me. It was the proverbial moment of truth. I knew I not only had to say something to that lady, but in so doing, I would also have to say something to Jacob about the Holocaust – not some abstract event of history that happened to others elsewhere, but a personal family horror that wiped out nearly all of his family tree.

I take off my seatbelt as the past and present converge in this moment I have anticipated before Jacob was even born. I glance at him. He radiates innocence. How do I say something without saying too much? How do I speak of *some* suffering, *some* death, when there was so much suffering and so much death? To protect him, I must find a way to say just a little. But a little that would mean something. I owe that to those whose lives have been extinguished and to those who survived. "I'll be right back, Jacob. I just want to say a few words to that lady inside." "What? What's the matter?" "It's okay, " I say reassuringly. "I'll explain in a minute. You can watch me from here. I won't be long."

I gathered myself as I walked inside and began calmly, "Excuse me. I was wondering if you realized what a Jewish star in yellow means, what it symbolizes?" "You know, I was thinking about that. Do you think it would be better if I painted it in white?"

Was her question about aesthetics or was there some vague sense of history in it?

I briefly explained the reference and that seeing it might evoke pain for some people, suggesting that any other color would be fine, white and blue traditionally used to represent Israel. She thanked me and said she appreciated my calling this to her attention. "I wouldn't want to offend anybody."

"What happened? What did you say to her? Why is she wiping off the yellow?" Jacob asked with curiosity when I returned. He doesn't know horror or evil yet. Sure, he's felt bad, has had his feelings hurt, but his world is full of compassion and understanding and trust. I don't want to shake any of that.

I begin gently and matter-of-factly. "When Grandma and Grandpa were teenagers, Jews had to wear yellow stars on the outside of their jackets." They were in their late 20s actually, I thought, but Jacob knew about teenagers from watching reruns of "Happy Days." "And many people treated them very mean and some were even killed."

"Some were even killed?" That glaring understatement continued to reverberate in my head. The "some" that were killed were grandparents I never knew, aunts, uncles, cousins I never got to meet and have as part of my life. My parents' entire world of European Jewry essentially ceased to exist as 6 million Jewish faces, including over 1 million Jewish children like Jacob, were wiped off the face of this earth. The Holocaust also obliterated 5 million non-Jews, including gypsies, Serbs, Poles, intellectuals, homosexuals, Jehovah's Witnesses, the disabled. So many lives, communities, and cultures were eliminated, considered unworthy of living by one of the most civilized cultures on earth. The same culture that gave us Bach and Brahms whose piano pieces I have loved to play all my life.

As I'm telling Jacob a few simple words, I hear all the sentences I'm censoring while recalling what Mom and Dad and the few surviving relatives told me about what had happened to them and to those who "didn't come back," those who "remained in Auschwitz." With these words I, too, was protected. I'm grateful I didn't hear "butchered," "slaughtered," "starved," "murdered," "gassed."

I remembered the one sad word that summed it all up: *elpusztultak,* they perished, with the "sz" in Hungarian sounding as "s" in English, onomatopoetic to my child's ear for poof! They vanished, disappeared.

"Why did we leave Hungary?" I would ask every few years after we escaped. "We came to America because we wanted to give you and Henry a better life." Emigration was not explained in terms of family persecution and extermination. Mom and Dad were still too frightened even in America to talk openly about their experience of anti-Semitism as they focused on rebuilding their lives and tried to provide everything for Henry and me.

It took nearly four decades for us to begin to talk about it all. And now I am beginning the process with my own child, cautiously but with commitment to teach, to have him learn something about his past, about himself, and how he can act with compassion and courage in the world.

I return to our conversation. Since we had already spoken about relationships between blacks and whites, prompted by celebrating Martin Luther King, Jr's birthday in his preschool, I drew a parallel, echoing our discussions about how some white people mistreat black people and how color shouldn't make a difference. "Yeah, what's the difference? People are people," Jacob asserted in his no-nonsense way. Logically it made no sense to him that people – a unifying concept in his mind – would be treated differently from each other.

Finally, I said, "So, if people going to the bakery, like

Grandma and Grandpa and others who know about those times, see the yellow star, they might feel bad because it would remind them of those terrible times in the past."

We began to drive home silently. A couple of minutes later, Jacob declares, "I'm sure glad I wasn't even born then yet! I'm glad you and Daddy weren't born then either!" And a few minutes later he adds, "But yellow is a pretty color, isn't it, Mommy?" "Yes, and if you want to, you can color a Star of David in yellow, or whatever color you want, when we're at home. It's just that in a public place where other people see it, it might make people feel bad."

A few weeks later, a couple days before Chanukah, Jacob asked if he could have his coloring book present early. He was getting restless since Sophie had chickenpox and we couldn't go out much. As he began to color, he suddenly asked, "Is it okay if I color a star in yellow?" And before I could respond, he said, "Oh, never mind. I don't want to. I don't want to make Grandma and Grandpa feel bad."

He got it. He learned something. Who knows whether anything about Holocaust history per se, but surely something about the value of knowing that history. That it's important to care about others and how they feel. That it's important to respect others and that you don't intentionally make others feel bad. A good beginning, I thought, filled with pride for both of us.

*

A year or so later, I'm walking across a supermarket's parking lot. It's prime time, just before dinnertime, and lots of cars are pulling in and out. I take Jacob's hand and lift Sophie up in my arms for added safety. Suddenly, I see myself from the back and begin to have the image of all those women and children walking toward the gas chambers. A deep sadness overtakes me and my eyes well up with burning tears as an imploring wish comes over me: I hope that as they walked unknowingly to their deaths, the mothers were able to hold their children's hands and lift their children in their arms as I was doing now. I hope that the continuity of comfort would not be broken, that the mothers could continue being mothers to their children, and the children could continue feeling enveloped by their mother's love in those final moments of their lives.

When I related this experience to a few friends and colleagues, they were gripped by the horror of it, yet it wasn't horror for me. It was a moment of grief mixed with gratefulness. A moment of mourning for all the mothers and children, my aunts and little cousins, my father's teenage niece whose name I bear. And a moment of gratitude, that here I am, a member of a generation that wasn't supposed to have been born, here yet with another generation I am able to, at least in this moment, protect and nurture.

*

We are walking in the beautiful town of Salzburg, having left one of the refugee camps for an outing, and I'm holding my father's hand. It feels so warm and firm and big. I'm so happy walking with him holding his hand, and it's positively sparkling all around us. The sun is shining brightly, the deep snow is glistening everywhere and crunching loudly under my feet. I'm all bundled up though my cheeks and nose are cold. I feel so energized and alive and happy, and holding my father's warm, comforting hand.

Everyone, that is, all the Jews in the town where I was living, had been deported. The dirt road on which they left stretches into the distance toward the left. It is now empty. Not a soul remains but Dad and me. I know I have to hurry to catch up with them so as not to get lost.

I turn around and go toward the building where I was living in order to get some clothes to wear and take with me. Dad is no longer around. In the front of the building, there is some kind of café with only a few people in it, only those who work there. I go past it to get inside the building, through the entrance on the right. I go inside but find all the doors to our rooms locked. Everyone's bedrooms are in a row, like in a dormitory: mine, my kids', Mom and Dad's. I look around to find the security guard to open them. He comes, wearing a dark uniform, and unlocks the rooms.

I go from one room to another to find my clothes, pulling out dresser drawers. I put on various long pants, trying to decide which ones would be the most suitable to wear. I always seem to have this problem of what to wear, nothing being quite right, I say to myself. No, these leggings are too thin and too light colored, and would show the dirt right away. Better to wear my regular blue jeans that are more substantial and darker, or the black jeans. But the black ones look funny with the white tennis shoes I always wear.

Which shoes to wear then? The Rockport ones are newer and in better condition, but after a while, my feet get tired and hurt in them. Better to wear the older white Easy Spirit ones and take along the Rockports, because it'll be many years of hardship and I'll probably wear both of them out. I think about Mom's and Sárika néni's stories of their shoes in Auschwitz and other camps, wooden shoes in winter, stuffing newspaper in them for warmth. I become resigned to the fact that the ones I'm taking will not last through all the years of hardship I face, but I know I can only take one besides the pair I decide to put on.

I see a top to wear, scooped neck, long sleeves, a greyish purple. It's Mom's, I think, as she suddenly appears and wants right then to give it to me. But I see that it has many long rips coming down from the right shoulder. As I face myself and see myself wearing it, the rips are on the left side and look like they could have been ripped by someone with claws. Five parallel rips of different lengths, the same pattern as fingers on a hand. I watch Mom, see only her back, watch her looking at me wearing her blouse. She is on the same side as the rips on the blouse. She insists I wear it. I can always cover up the rips with a big pin, she says. I argue that's ridiculous, it's torn, and become agitated. I know the pin would never cover all of it up. Some of the rips would still show, coming down from under and around the pin. She argues back. Scene changes and I'm not wearing the blouse anymore.

While I continue to search around, trying quickly to decide what to wear and what to take, the guard is standing casually opposite me. He's just watching and waiting for me. He's not at all threatening. He's just waiting for me to finish so he can lock up again.

I turn to him and engage him in conversation to tell him what will happen. This is just the beginning of it and he has no clue. I say to him, protesting, "Do you know what's going to happen?! All these people have been taken away and very few will survive!" He listens with a serious look on his face.

I am preparing to go into the Holocaust with full knowledge of the horror that had happened during it. I am at once in the beginning of it and after it. I am rushing about trying to gather together what would be the most useful and durable clothes to take for such an ordeal, which pants would be the strongest, which shoes would be the most comfortable and last as long as possible, trying quickly to put them on and take an extra set in order to join the others who have already left. And I must catch up with them or else I will be lost.

I wake up instantly. Details of my dream swirl and pound inside me, demanding immediate attention. Trembling, I know I have just experienced something deep, sacred. I watch the images replay before me as messages burst forth with meaning.

My need to catch up with everyone is my need and sense of urgency to get the stories from the survivors in my family while they are still alive. Once they are gone, I fear I might be lost without them. I belong with them and perhaps should die off with them, too. Henry and I talk about not quite feeling second generation but rather in between, having one foot in each, the bridge between. Is it because we were born in the Old Country, speak that language, spent our childhood on the land where it all happened? Children born into the remnants of that world that no longer exists but which we often return to and long for.

I meet the challenge of being on their road head on and don't want to conceal anything. I don't want to cover up the rips on the blouse my mother insists I wear. Her scars and pain cannot be covered up, so she tries to hide them as best she can and go on. I haven't received those scars directly, so I have the luxury to immerse myself completely in them, make some sense of them, transform them into something positive and hopeful for myself. My parents have Faith I cannot feel, but somehow I must find another way to reconcile that which no one can understand, but all of us who inherited the Holocaust directly from our parents must live with.

I prepare to follow and join them on a journey whose tragic outcome I already know, yet I don't question whether to go or not, have no thoughts of hiding or escaping. I want to go, but why am I not afraid? There is a sense of belonging in sorting through the bones of my past and a sense of mastery meeting it head on. I am determined to accompany them on this journey I must do in order to know them and the world I come from, and to ultimately know myself.

15

Searching for the Commanding Officer's name, honoring him as a Righteous Among the Nations

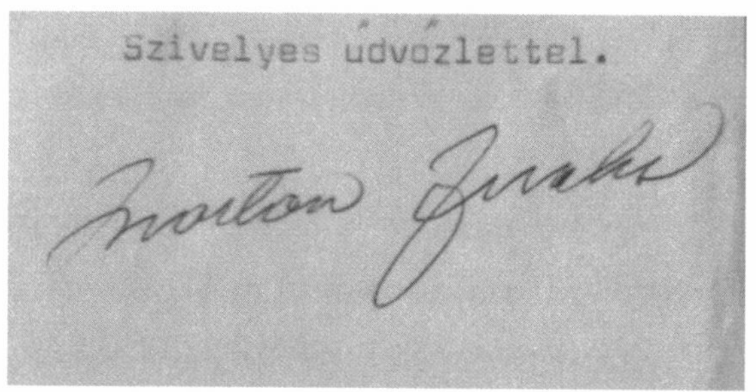
Szivelyes üdvözlettel.

It was while helping Dad prepare for a 1987 televised interview of our family that he first recounted the details of his labor camp years. As he started telling me about the Commanding Officer who had saved his life, he was embarrassed and ashamed that he could not remember his name, and therefore didn't want to talk about him for the program. "It was 40 years ago," I offered. "It's understandable one would forget a name." My words provided little comfort as he continued to shake his head. "But here is his picture." He pulled from his files an old envelope in which was the little black and white photograph he had received decades ago from the Commanding Officer's wife and which he had packed along with the barest of essentials when we escaped from Hungary. Never before had I seen this picture nor knew anything about these extraordinary circumstances.

Stunned, I turned to Dad with resolve. "We must find out his name and have him honored at Yad Vashem as a Righteous Gentile." In the midst of all the horror, this one man acted at great personal peril to save his fellow human beings. The world must know.

Dad began writing. Perhaps one of his labor camp friends would remember, perhaps Isaac Guttman in New York or Sanyi Frankel in Budapest. A few months later, both of them wrote back. Unfortunately, neither could remember the name of their Commanding Officer but sent their own recollections testifying to his goodness. Sanyi Frankel also mentioned that he had contacted Jenö Goldstein who had been the cook in their labor battalion. Perhaps he would remember the name.

Several months passed, and one night Dad called to say he had received a letter that day. Their Commanding Officer's name was Zoltán Kubinyi.

We quickly prepared the documentation to submit to Yad Vashem, the Holocaust Memorial & Museum in Jerusalem that honors rescuers of Jews during the Holocaust. We also translated Isaac Guttman's testimony in Hungarian and included it as a required second witness:

A couple days before we were liberated, we were marching on a country road in Hungary. For a few minutes we stopped to rest. I took out my tfillin and put it on and started to pray. Suddenly, the order came to resume marching. I didn't take off my tfillin, but I asked those men around me to surround me closer so that the oncoming group of German military coming toward us would not see me. Many men said this was dangerous because I was endangering the entire group. Word about this reached our Commanding Officer Zoltán Kubinyi, and he didn't order me to take off the tfillin. Instead, he got off the covered wagon he was riding on and let me sit in his place until I finished my daily prayers while he marched alongside the men.

A day before we were liberated, the cooking was very disorganized. Zoltán Kubinyi was looking for me to make sure I had food to eat. He brought me some cooked potatoes because he knew and respected that I, being a very religious man, didn't eat from the regular food.

He was a very religious Seventh Day Adventist and many times we used to discuss together passages from the Bible. On his holster around his waist, he never wore the pistol that he was supposed to because it was forbidden to carry weapons according to his religious beliefs."

Isaac Lipe

(Isaac Guttman's Hebrew name)

In his February 1988 letter to Yad Vashem, Dad detailed the events that took place under Kubinyi's command and summed up his testimony with the following words:

"Zoltán Kubinyi was a true human being in the deepest sense of the word. During this catastrophic event, when civilized, intelligent people were blinded with irrational hatred, and innocent people, mothers with babies in their arms were slaughtered, HE WAS A MAN. Risking his own life, he stood up for and defended the innocent, persecuted people.

The memory of Zoltán Kubinyi deserves the highest honor that a person could possibly deserve for his altruistic, heroic, and self-sacrificing activities."

Morton Fuchs

(Dad's name was changed from Miksa to Morton when we became American citizens in 1962)

In early April 1990, Dad and I each received the letter from Yad Vashem that we had been anxiously waiting for:

Jerusalem, 27 March 1990

RE: Kubinyi, Zoltán -- (4558)

We are happy to inform you, that at its last meeting on 12.2.1990 the Commission for the Designation of the Righteous decided to confer upon the above person the title of Righteous Among the Nations. This recognition includes the right to a medal of honour and the privilege of having his name inscribed in the Garden of the Righteous, at Yad Vashem, Jerusalem.

Sincerely yours,

Dr. Mordecai Paldiel
Director, Dept. for the Righteous

Over the next few years, we tried searching for Zoltán Kubinyi's wife and son. I wanted to meet them and thank them for Dad's life and therefore my own. Because of Zoltán Kubinyi, Hitler's "Final Solution to the Jewish Question," nearly foolproof in extinguishing the Jews of Europe, failed to work completely. Over 100 men were saved, and as a result, members of a generation that wasn't supposed to have been born, like Henry and me, had the chance to be. I also wanted to find them so they would know that Zoltán Kubinyi had been honored by Yad Vashem, and for them to receive the certificate and medallion from Jerusalem.

The last Dad had heard, Kubinyi's wife and son had moved from Budapest to Miskolc. On the trip back to

Hungary in 1991, I looked in the phone book that was by the pay phone in the back of a Miskolc restaurant we had stopped in for lunch and started calling the Kubinyis listed. Those who answered either said, sorry, there's no Zoltán Kubinyi in our family, or simply hung up annoyed. Unfortunately, we had to leave Hungary before I could finish calling the two dozen or so names, but our friends Miki and Judit in Tokaj kindly offered to continue.

A few months later, I received a letter from Judit. She had found the family and had spoken with the son's wife. He was at work. Sadly, his mother had passed away a year or so before. "She never believed that her husband had died and spent her days praying and waiting for him to come back."

Dad immediately wrote to the son, sending him a copy of the documentation in his original Hungarian. A short time later, the son replied and sent as verification a copy of his father's identity card showing the same photograph Dad had shown me. Alongside it was a copy of his own identity card with a picture of a man resembling his father.

As I looked into the eyes of Márton Gábor Kubinyi, only six months old when his father went off to war, never to return, I wondered what it must have been like for him to not know his father and now learn, nearly 50 years later, how much his father means to others.

Dear Mr. Fuchs!

I was deeply moved by the fact that an American newspaper, even if it is only a relatively small group's paper, would like to tell my late father's story.

My father was baptized in Barcelona on June 30, 1937, prepared by Brother Struve, and became a member of the Seventh Day Adventist Church. These were hard times during the Civil War in Spain. There were hardly 2,000 members of the community. In 1942 he returned home and became a book evangelist of the Hungarian Church. Then he worked as a secretary in the religion department. He worked there until he got his call to be a soldier. He met my mother in this community and they married in 1943 in the month of January in the denomination headquarters, Székély Bertalán Street Chapel.

I was born on 20 November 1943. My father joined up in May 1944, served as a warrant officer due to his qualifications, but he saved the group he was in charge of, according to his belief and lifestyle.

This was not appreciated by the victors, and as a Hungarian prisoner of war he is resting in an anonymous grave. His death was never confirmed. My mother until her death in 1988 expected him back.

Once again I am very happy that you looked for me and I had the opportunity to tell you the reality in a few words. I hope you are in good health. My warm regards to your dear daughter and son.

*

I thank you and I am deeply touched for your doing everything tirelessly to immortalize the memory of my father.

*

I received your kind letter in which you tell me that you are going to get in touch again with Yad Vashem. Once again, thank you for your efforts and your kind mediation.

I was touched when I read the testimony about my father. He had this kind of soul, indeed, according to what my mother told as well. She did not want to believe that he is not here anymore. She waited for him until her death in 1988. She never used the term widow with her name. Unfortunately, she could not live to see this glorious moment. I am deeply touched and I am proud that my father lived this way and acted by which he earned the distinction of true, righteous person. Thank you very much for your dedication to this case.

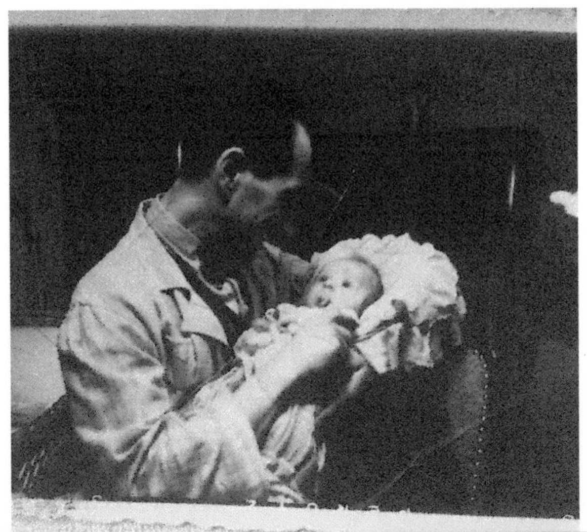

Márton Kubinyi
with father Zoltán & mother Sarolta (Pöstényi) Kubinyi

Budapest, 1943 and 1944

In February 1994, in a nationally televised ceremony in Budapest, Márton Gábor Kubinyi received from a representative from Yad Vashem the Certificate and Medallion of Honor on behalf of his father, posthumously honored as Righteous Among the Nations.

Zoltán Kubinyi's name had also been inscribed on a wall in the Garden of the Righteous at Yad Vashem in Jerusalem.

Márton Gábor Kubinyi (*right*), Budapest, February 1994

16

Holocaust Commemoration
Tokaj, 1994

During our visit in 1990 with the Mayor of Tokaj, János Májer, Henry mentioned that in 1994 it will be 50 years that the Jews of Tokaj were rounded up. It would be fitting to have some kind of commemoration to honor them.

The Mayor leaped up and declared, “Yes! We must do this and we will!” Henry and I looked at each other with relief and gratitude.

Four years later by phone and letters, with the Mayor and his staff, and our childhood friends Miki and Lajcsi, we planned the program. The date would be in May to coincide with Shavuos, the Jewish holiday on which day in 1944 the Jews of Tokaj arrived in Auschwitz. Among them were Noémi and Judit, Dad's brother Vilmos' daughters, whose photograph Henry used for the poster announcing the Commemoration. I indicated that I wanted to speak about Zoltán Kubinyi and invite his son so that we could honor him for his father's heroic deeds.

On the way to Hungary, Henry and I stopped in London and visited Peter, Mom's cousin who as a teenager survived by hiding with his family in a farmhouse on the outskirts of Budapest. Peter decided to join us for the Commemoration. He was going to Budapest anyway to attend Jutka's son Tamás's wedding. Jutka had survived with her family hiding in a "safe house" in Budapest. After the wedding, Peter, Henry, and I drove down to Tokaj. Jutka took the train the following day, arriving just in time for the 4pm program.

As we embraced at the Tokaj station, I recalled how in '56 we had tearfully said goodbye to Jutka and her parents, Manci *néni* and Jenö *bácsi*. I thought of the time when Mom and Dad would no longer be alive and Jutka, Henry, and I would be meeting each other then. As the youngest of the survivors with Peter and Éva, who lives in Montreal, Jutka will be one of the few links to our past and the only relative born before the war who is still living in Hungary.

*

Over 200 people gathered on the top floor of the Tokaj Synagogue, under reconstruction to be a cultural center, for the first Holocaust Commemoration ever held in the town. Aside from the few Jews remaining in Tokaj today and a handful of survivors who came from nearby towns, the majority present were the non-Jewish townspeople.

Why did they come? Partly out of curiosity, I imagined, partly because it was a big event in a small town, and partly to mourn the loss of their Jewish friends and neighbors who before the war had comprised almost a quarter of the town's population.

Everyone was formally dressed and an air of solemnity and anticipation filled the room. Photographs of Tokaj Jews who had perished, including members of our family, lined the wall. Next to them was the photograph of Zoltán Kubinyi. As I started to look at all the faces, I realized I had seen most of them before. With hundreds of others, these photos were randomly piled in a cardboard box that was sitting by the counter in our friend Lajcsi's little clothing store when we visited in 1990. As I was looking through stack after stack of photos, an oddly familiar face appeared in my hand. "What's this doing here?" stunned I asked. It was my first school picture from America, New Jersey 1957. "Irenke *néni* you sent it to said I should keep it." Mom had sent the photo to our beloved music teacher who had been teaching me piano and Henry the violin.

Though shocked to see myself amidst all those whose lives were brutally extinguished, it somehow felt fitting. Afterall, I, too, was a Tokaj Jew, born into the remnants of their once thriving Jewish community. I felt a deep sense of solidarity with them, and by looking into each of their faces, I felt I was helping to keep them alive.

Next to the photos on display in the Synagogue were half a dozen Martyr lists, the names of those in the photos and other Tokaj Jews who didn't survive. Sheets of blank paper, evoking their vanished existence, were placed beneath each list for possible additions and corrections by people assembled here today.

As a television crew was setting up lights, and musicians from a local music academy were tuning up, Henry and I took our seats in the front row with the other speakers. Our cousin Peter said he and Jutka would sit in the back so they could leave, if necessary, before the program was finished, in order to catch the 5:30pm train back to Budapest.

Several people who knew us as kids came up to greet us and sent their love to Mom and Dad. Laci Lazarovits, Mom's friend she had spoken about who was the police captain after the war, remarked, "I'm glad to see that the most beautiful woman in Tokaj had a likewise beautiful daughter." He handed me a copy of a poem he had written when he visited Auschwitz a few years back and asked me to give it to Mom and Dad.

As 4 o'clock came and went, we kept wondering why the program wasn't starting and asked Gisella, the charming and efficient woman from City Hall who was in charge. "The men from Debrecen are waiting for more Jewish men to come so they could begin with prayers." Out of the more than 200 people already there, including a dozen standing in the aisles, we were waiting for merely a *minyan*, a quorum of 10 Jewish men required for public prayer. This alone spoke volumes about the very reason we were there.

Finally around 4:15, Rabbi Moskovitz from Debrecen walked up to the microphone and began. "Since this is a special occasion and we are in the newly restored Synagogue, and since there are enough men, it is fitting that we start with *Mariv*, the afternoon service. Will those men who are of the Jewish faith who are wearing *yarmulkes,* as well as those who are not wearing them, please come up and join me for the prayers?"

I counted as 11 men, including Henry, Miki, Lajcsi, Peti, and Laci walked up to the front and stood next to the rabbi and faced the audience. I looked at our friend Peti whose beautifully crafted jewelry I wear, and thought about his father Gyula *bácsi* Henry and I knew and who has passed away. I was remembering that Dad and Gyula *bácsi's* younger brother were in labor camp together, and watching Peti I kept picturing the scenes Mom and Sárika *néni* related of Gyula *bácsi* throwing his handkerchief to Mom in Auschwitz to cover up his sister's bald head, the same sister whose family photographs Sárika *néni* tried to save between her sanitary pads. Neither the photos nor Gyula' *bácsi's* sister survived.

As the rabbi *davened*, some of the men like Henry who knew the prayers by heart joined in, but most of them stood there silently. Many had long ago stopped praying, for a variety of reasons I imagined, both personal and communal. The rabbi's body was bobbing and bending in traditional ways, and for parts of prayers he took steps in different directions in the fashion familiar to those of us raised in religious communities. I wondered how the non-Jews present felt seeing this, particularly the younger generation who might have never met any Jews, let alone religious ones, nor known of the vibrant Jewish life that once flourished in their own community.

How many decades had it been since this century old Synagogue had reverberated with the ancient sounds of Hebrew? I felt uncomfortable hearing it so publicly uttered in front of an audience. But perhaps this is the closest thing to a real service that would be held here, with a congregation of stand-ins for those souls who were killed for believing in these very words.

Some speeches followed, the first one by the Mayor who welcomed everyone and spoke about missing the Jews of Tokaj. The history professor, István Zelenák, spoke methodically with details and statistics about the history of the Tokaj Jews. The Head of the Holocaust commission from Budapest spoke in formal Hungarian that Henry and I couldn't fully understand, but his outrage needed no translation. Interspersed was classical music beautifully played by the academy's students and faculty. Irénke *néni*, our music teacher sitting next to me, and I exchanged appreciative glances. Yet I longed for Yiddish and Hebrew melodies to infuse this holy place with a sense of Jewishness missing in the melodies of the masters.

Finally, it is my turn to speak. I cannot keep the papers of my speech from shaking in my hands as I stand before the bare microphone. My lips and throat run dry, and complete silence falls as I begin to tell the story of a man who rescued some men, some of the only Jewish men from this town who survived.

As I finish relating the events of the past and announce that Márton Gábor Kubinyi recently received the commendation on behalf of his father, everyone bursts into applause that spontaneously becomes rhythmic, indicating a wish for him to stand up. The Mayor in the front row throws me a worried look, "Is he here?" With all the frenzy of preparations, no one had remembered to check if the rescuer's son had even arrived. I shrug my shoulders glancing at the Mayor, finish the last line of my speech, and taking a chance, ask if Márton Gábor Kubinyi would please stand up.

Everyone turns their head with great anticipation, but we see no one. Finally, way in the back a man's head slowly appears, barely visible above the crowd. Suddenly, I'm torn. I want to march straight back and shake his hand and say thank you, thank you for your father, thank you for helping me believe there is goodness in the world. But it would take so long to walk all the way back to him. Can I burden everyone by doing so? Would this be doing something solely for me, or restorative to others as well, others who may need bolstering of faith in people in the midst of all this Holocaust horror? The vastness of space lies ahead of me, yet I feel the immediacy of those events pushing me to reach out for the goodness this man represents.

I try to soften the clicking of my heels as I move across the concrete floor and try to contain the feelings swirling within me. I can barely breathe. This is a moment in history. A punctuation of events that happened 50 years ago.

I approach the son and look into his eyes, likewise filled with tears, and think: Neither of us knew your father, but both our lives have been defined by him. We shake hands, and he leans down and kisses mine in the age-old tradition of gentility. “I am happy to meet you. We will talk afterwards at the dinner,” I say softly.

Speeches continued. The Debrecen rabbi spoke emotionally about the losses of the Holocaust, and more music was gracefully performed. Finally, two hours later, Gisella poignantly closed the program, “It is now beginning to rain, as if to shed tears.” She asked everyone to convene outside with the Mayor to unveil the memorial tablet and put up the wreath to commemorate this 50th anniversary of the destruction of Hungarian Jews.

As people were departing, more friends of Mom and Dad came up to greet Henry and me, sharing memories of our family. In the midst of all this sorrow and loss, everyone seemed hungry and grateful for the connection of friends and some semblance of a lost Jewish community.

The Synagogue emptied and I walked over to the windows to have a moment alone. Through the portholes I watched the crowd below listening to the Mayor with the memorial wreath in his hands. I looked over at the stork nest perched on the wooden pole across the street, the nest that has been there ever since I was born and probably for decades before. Only now, to my delight, did I see baby storks in it for the first time. As I looked with fascination at them, I wondered: Did *their* ancestors watch *my* ancestors get herded like cattle into this Synagogue and live on its grounds for a week and then completely disappear? Did they wonder where all those people went? Did they think they were migrating to Africa, too, and would return just like *they* do every year?

Needing to get to the special dinner with the Mayor and anxious to speak with Kubinyi's son, I quickly started walking down the stairs past Henry who was helping an elderly woman survivor who had traveled from a town hours away. She was painfully taking one laborious step after another with her walker. "I'm so glad I came and could see you two," she tearfully told us earlier. "It took her a whole hour to walk up here to the top floor," Henry later remarked.

*

"I want to thank you for your father. I am here in this world because of what he did in saving *my* father. But *you* didn't have a father to love you and raise you like *I* had."

My words in Hungarian came out haltingly as I tried to express my gratitude mixed with sorrow for the loss of his father as well as the hardships that he, a fatherless child after the war, must have had to endure. A myriad of questions I had long wanted to ask him clamored in my head as I fought my instinct to protect him and not intrude.

Had he known any of this about his father before he received Dad's letter about our application to Yad Vashem to honor his father? How much had he already known from letters his mother received just after the war from Dad and the other labor camp men who sent the care packages to them?

Yes, he had known about the events during the war, not from letters his mother received from the labor camp men, instead from a few soldiers who came back from captivity in Russia, bringing back his father's dog tags. But his mother never got official notification of his father's death. Only recently, when they appealed to the Hungarian government for some restitution, did they find out that his father had died from typhus. The Red Cross had helped in getting the information and verification.

How did he feel when he received Dad's letter and what his friend Isaac Guttman also wrote about his father? "I cried right away," his wife immediately answered. I can't remember what, if anything, the son said, but I recall thinking he must have been filled with mixed emotions, emotions that defy expression in words.

"He was very angry at times that he didn't have a father, that his mother quit her job, and as a result, he had to quit school and start working at age 14," his wife explained. "And his mother became quite fanatical, praying all the time for her husband's return." A bus driver in Miskolc for many years, "He has worked hard all his life. That's how he knows how to do everything," the wife proudly stated, "like all the various aspects to building that we are doing on our house. And I do the letter writing he doesn't like to do," she added chuckling.

With the clanging of utensils and platters being passed around, and several conversations going on around us, it was difficult to hear everything the son and his wife were saying. Some of the Hungarian was also hard for me to understand. As I listened with Henry sitting next to me, also earnestly asking questions, it felt like listening through a veil, trying to understand each word that was partly hidden, and between the words each space that vibrated with possibility of meaning too overwhelming to assimilate.

Finally, I asked the crucial question that had been haunting me for years: Why didn't your father take off his uniform and save himself as he had saved so many others?

Was it honor? Honor as a military officer and a deeply religious man? Was it pride? Pride in using his Nazi-allied uniform for the higher good? Did he really believe that nothing would happen to him? That the Russians would follow the Geneva Convention protocols for humane treatment of prisoners of war? (As it turned out, chief among those nations that did not adhere to the 1929 Convention were Russia and Japan.) Or did he say that nothing would happen to him in order to reassure his men? Was it principle above pragmatics? That his fundamental respect for others, the honesty, integrity, and conviction that must have compelled him to act with such courage to rescue others, transcended any consideration for himself and his family?

I offered some of these thoughts as we became locked in a mystery that was unsolvable yet full of consequence. Finally, the son answered, simply and with resignation, as if he had made peace with it all.

"I, too, have often thought about this question. I think he didn't take off his uniform because he was such a religious man, was always honest, never lied. And to do so would be to lie. He hadn't done anything wrong, so why should he take off his uniform?"

We looked at each other, trying to absorb those events of the past and the repercussions they have had on our lives. Silently, they pulled out the certificate of commendation and the heavy silver medallion and placed them before Henry and me. As I started to pass them around to others at the table, the wife reached into her purse and took out a photograph. It showed Zoltán Kubinyi with his wife. A lovely young couple, smiling and looking radiant. "Please have this from us," she said to me.

Blinking away tears, I could barely see the picture in my hands. A happy life together, unjustly interrupted forever. "Oh, no, I cannot accept this, if it is your only copy." "No," she reassured me, "we have another one. Please take it."

כאילו קיים עולם מלא ... WORLD

בזכירה סוד הגאולה
Remembrance is the Secret of Redemption
(Baal Shem Tov)

תעודת כבוד
Certificate of Honour

THIS IS TO CERTIFY THAT IN ITS SESSION OF FEBRUARY 12, 1990 THE COMMISSION FOR THE DESIGNATION OF THE RIGHTEOUS, ESTABLISHED BY YAD VASHEM, THE HOLOCAUST HEROES & MARTYRS' REMEMBRANCE AUTHORITY, ON THE BASIS OF EVIDENCE PRESENTED BEFORE IT, HAS DECIDED TO HONOUR

Zoltan Kubinyi

WHO, DURING THE HOLOCAUST PERIOD IN EUROPE, RISKED HIS LIFE TO SAVE PERSECUTED JEWS.
THE COMMISSION, THEREFORE, HAS ACCORDED HIM THE MEDAL OF THE RIGHTEOUS AMONG THE NATIONS.
HIS NAME SHALL BE FOREVER ENGRAVED ON THE HONOUR WALL IN THE GARDEN OF THE RIGHTEOUS, AT YAD VASHEM, JERUSALEM.

Jerusalem, Israel
JANUARY 24, 1993

את לתעודה שבישיבתה
ום יז שבט תש״ן
חליטה הועדה לציון
סידי אומות העולם
ליד רשות הזיכרון יד ושם
יסוד עדויות
הובאו לפניה, לתת כבוד
ר ל

לטן קוביניי

אשר בשנות השואה
אירופה שם נפשו בכפו
הצלת יהודים נרדפים
רודפיהם ולהעניק לו
המדליה לחסידי אומות
עולם.
יונצח לעד על לוח-
ר בחורשת חסידי אומות
עולם ביד ושם.

היום בירושלים
שבט תשנ״ג

Zoltán Kubinyi and his wife Sarolta Pöstényi
on the occasion of their engagement

Budapest, 1942

I have shown the picture and told the story of Zoltán Kubinyi to my children: This is the man who saved your Grandpa's life. You, too, like him, can act with courage and goodness. Though hatred and prejudice still permeate the world, you can make a difference. His example can provide you with some comfort and inspiration, as it does for me. And it can give you hope for creating a better world to come.

17

Dad's letters from the hospital

In March of 2000, Dad was in and out of the hospital getting lasix treatments for water retention due to congestive heart failure. For months he would say, "I'm fine except I am so tired and so weak."

He would sleep more and I noticed he'd often close his eyes when he ate.

Early one morning, as soon as I came into his hospital room, he sat up and exclaimed, "Something remarkable happened last night! I want you to write a letter for me." He dictated it and asked me to give it to the nurse supervisor.

I'm staying here in the hospital. All the nurses are very helpful, nice, and polite. They have taken my blood many times. Unfortunately, it is very hard to find the veins on my arms, so the nurses have great difficulty doing it and have to try three or four places before they find a place that will work.

This one young man, Fred Brown, in the middle of last night, looked at both my arms and immediately found a spot. He put in the needle so gently that I didn't even feel it. He found the vein right away and the blood began to flow.

I couldn't believe it and I told him, "Never has anybody found it so easily and painlessly and right away. Thank you so much. I admire you for how well you did it."

Morton Fuchs
March 4, 2000

The following day, we talked about how wonderful it was that he could be at Jacob's Bar Mitzvah, held in our home three years earlier. I told him how much it meant to me and to all of us what he said to Jacob and that he blessed him. There wasn't a dry eye in the house as we witnessed the emotional interchange.

What would he say to the *other* grandchildren on the

occasion of *their* Bar/Bat Mitzvahs? Unspoken was our shared sorrow that he probably would not live to see those days. If he wished, I could jot down some notes as he thought out loud about it.

He liked the idea. "Let's do it," and he suggested that he dictate his messages in Hungarian, I would translate them, and together we could later make changes, after which he would read each message into the tape recorder so the kids could have an audio copy. "Be sure to buy 4 tapes!" "It's a good thing you said that," I laughed, "because I only thought of bringing 1 tape! You're way ahead of me!"

He took a long deep breath, and the words began to flow almost flawlessly, and in English. By the gaze in his eyes, by his whole presence, you could see that he was standing before each grandchild, speaking directly from his heart to each one of them he considered special and loved so much.

He started with Sam who he knew was already learning the blessings and his Haftorah. By the time he came to Jacob, he was exhausted but continued. When he finished he said, "That's enough for now," and turned to sleep. It was the last time he was so energetic. He never had the chance to dictate into the taperecorder.

Samuel,

One of my favorite grandsons, Samuel Mintzer Fuchs, Shlomo Ben Y'Hezkel ve Mashe Shena.

I love you so much.

There is two more years to your Bar Mitzvah and I like to be there so much. I am old and sick, going to be 89, and I do everything to keep healthy. I watch myself, taking care of my health, I follow the doctors' directions, and I hope I will be there and share the simcha with our family at your Bar Mitzvah.

But we never know what might happen from one day to the other. I hope I will make it. But if not, I would like to leave a message to you, Samike.

You know, during my old age, I saw a lot and experienced a lot. And I have kind of ideas how to live happily and peaceful:

Be friendly to everybody. If someone needs some help and you can help, I'm sure you will help them.

Love your parents very much.

And your sister, Miriam – always support her, be with her, go places together somewhere, enjoy each other.

And love your Grandmothers, Bubbie and Nagymama, and respect them, all your relatives.

And the most important, you study. Study hard and everything is good to know. You never know when it comes handy. Everything you can learn how to do it and what to do. Read books, what is useful. From books you can learn a lot. The education is the most important in life.

Remember people and never wait for anybody to say hello. You greet people first.

I think if you will do this kind of lifestyle, you will be a very happy person.

Someday you going to meet a nice Jewish girl and you going to get married. You going to have children. Explain for the children. Give them the best education and explain for your children the education is the most important and the best investment in life. Education gives you knowledge, power, people respect you, and you will be very happy.

Samuka, I'm sure you going to make it in life. You are so smart, intelligent, friendly, good personality, and you will be somebody. And the whole world is going to know you.

That's my message. I hope I can tell you this personally on your Bar Mitzvah.

*

Dear Sophieka,

I love you so much.

You remember your Hebrew name is Yehudit Bas Yisroel ve Frimet, your father's and mother's Hebrew names.

I love you so much.

There is almost two years if you want to be Bas Mitzvahed. I like to be there so much. I give you this message what I'm going to tell you on tape.

As I told Sammy, I want to tell you, too. I'm old and sick and I do everything to reach this day. But we never know what happens from one day to the other. If I would make it, I like to say and give you some message:

You're so talented, so intelligent, and so nice, so friendly. I enjoy your company always so much. It's so good to hug you. You're such a sweet girl.

Take your education, and I know it's hard for you to study. Force yourself because education is the most important.

I see some talents in you, drawing, continue. Maybe you can learn more from some professional because you never know what's going to be in the future and you have to make a living.

Love your brother and accept his help and advice because he's so smart and has more experience.

Love your parents. They are fine people. They raised you and you became a beautiful, intelligent, smart girl.

Love your relatives.

Be friendly and polite to everybody. Never wait for people to say hello. You say hello to everybody, your friends, relatives, whoever you know.

Sometime you going to meet a nice young man and you going to be married. You going to have children. Teach your children about this advice I give you. And you really give them the best education. The best education is the best investment and best thing in life because education is power, people will love you, ask your advice, people will respect you.

Love your Grandmother. If she needs some help, support her.

And I hope you going to have a beautiful, happy life.

And I love you, Sophieka, so much.

*

Miriamka,

My dear granddaughter, I love you so much.

As you know, Miriam is a Hebrew name and your father's name is Y'Hezkel and your mother's name is Mashe Shena.

You're very intelligent and very independent. You don't wait for others to do something for you. If you want something, you do it yourself and I love that.

Maybe you're too young if I give you some message, some advice what to do in life. Maybe you wouldn't quite understand:

You just continue studying in school and learn things how to do.

I know you like to do everything by yourself, but sometimes everybody needs some help what to do. Ask your brother, your father, your mother, your uncles, but don't hesitate to ask people.

You're so friendly to people. I'm sure you're going to be friendly all your life and everybody will love you.

Love your relatives, your uncles, and occasionally write them a nice letter or greeting card. If you have something nice, give a little present to people.

And I hope you going to have a very happy, nice happy life.

Love, your Nagypapa who loves you so much.

*

Jacobka,

You're one of our prides of the family, the oldest one among our grandchildren, who the entire family is proud of.

You have a good personality, you are kind to people, to your friends, you are kind to your parents.

Now that I have left a message for the other grandchildren, I would like to leave something for you also so that you will remember your grandfather.

There is two more years and you going to go to college. By that time, you going to have your own car and you going to be absolutely independent.

First of all, very careful how you drive. Observe the rules. I'm sure you going to know every detail of the driving rules.

Be careful with your friends. Don't associate with bad people. Don't try to help them, don't try to do anything with them. Make sure all your friends are intelligent, responsible people and it won't cause you any trouble, problems. Love them, get together, study together, spend time together, go places together, enjoy life.

What you study is the most important. I don't know what you going to be. How I understand, at this time the children really don't know what they're going to do. But there going to pop up something what you like to do.

And what you do, take it with good feeling. I love to do it, and you do the work.

If you going to do some work and have a boss, be respectful and follow his advice and directions.

Sometime you going to have your own company. Be reasonable with people.

And sometime, as I told all my grandchildren, you going to meet a nice girl, get married, have children. And pass on this message from your Grandpa who loves you so much.

You did your Bar Mitzvah ceremony so well, so well done that everyone was so proud of you.

18

The Last time I saw Dad

one of Dad's violins and favorite red carnation

A couple days later, on Wednesday afternoon at the convalescent home, I had to say goodbye to Dad. Having been in the hospital with him since the previous week, I needed to return to my kids and back to work now that he was stable and improving.

It hurt me to see my proud, independent, and competent father in this facility filled with folks more impaired physically and cognitively, but he was not strong enough to go directly home, especially since it would be too hard physically for Mom to help him. As we talked and he rested, he said he needed to use the bathroom. He pushed his call button for assistance, needing help getting out of bed and walking to the restroom. More than ten minutes slowly and painfully elapsed and still no one came. My own attempts to halt someone in the hallway yielded no one. Finally a woman came in, admonishing and irritated at repeated urgings of the ringer. "We can always put diapers on you so that you don't need to be uncomfortable waiting." Shock and dismay washed over Dad's face and mine. She could have been well meaning, but her words felt like an assault to Dad's dignity. Slowly and softly he replied, "No, I can use the toilet. I just need help getting there."

As Dad came back to bed, it was more apparent just how tired and weak he was. I wished I didn't have to leave before he was home safe and sound. I started to lean down to hug and kiss him but couldn't reach over the bars high up on both sides of the bed. I didn't want to keep him awake any longer by trying to figure out where the lever was and how it worked. I got up on my tiptoes, stretched and leaned over but still could not reach to fully hug him. So I kissed him gently on his forehead, then his right cheek and left, ending with a peck on the top of his nose. He smiled gently as he looked into my eyes, enjoying the playfulness.

Suddenly, I noticed his olive skin, exactly like mine, unlike Mom's and Henry's. I was surprised by what I already knew. We really *are* the same physically and temperamentally. "Sleep well and I'll talk to you tonight" I said, trying to counteract my reluctance to leave. He closed his eyes and fell asleep instantly.

Little did I know this would be the last time I would see him. Though he had been very sick, he always rallied, and it seemed impossible to imagine he wouldn't again. Perhaps denial had set in, for it did not even occur to me that I wouldn't see him again, robust and energetic as usual.

Two days later he asked to be taken home, his patience completely worn by the lack of timely care at the nursing home. I wasn't surprised and felt relieved. That evening he got up for *Shabbes*, quietly *davened*, and led Mom, Henry, and a couple friends in singing *Shalom Aleichem* in his usual strong, beautiful tenor voice. His last *Shabbes* was joyous as always.

19

Dad's passing and his funeral

Henry

"Don't bother Henry. He was up late last night." Dad's last words. I'm half-asleep in Marta's old room, Monday morning, March 13, 2000. Dad is just outside the door, on the way to the shower, assisted by a young aide. A minute later, I hear her scream. I jump out of bed, rush into the bathroom. She's standing outside the shower and Dad has fainted, slumped into the corner of the shower stall. I say "call 911," turn off the shower, and try to haul him out.

He's very wet and slippery, one faint gurgle the only sign of life. I keep trying to get him out, he keeps slipping away, totally limp. I have him mostly out when a 911 respondent comes to take over. I say, "He doesn't want heroic measures, doesn't want to live on a machine," as I rush out to change from pajamas to clothes so I can go with the ambulance to the hospital. A minute later, I'm tying my shoes, a responder comes into my room. "No need to rush," he says, "we couldn't save him." The world stops. I don't know for how long. "Where shall we put him?" "I guess on the bed, " I reply.

Only a few days ago Dad was released from the hospital to a nursing home next door to the synagogue. But he couldn't tolerate being there. They weren't sure that when he signaled, they could get an assistant in time to help him to the toilet, so they proposed he wear a diaper, "just in case." Get me out of here, he asked Mom. So she did. We started interviewing aides to help him at home.

Saturday Dad was still too weak to go to services, but he was up and sitting in the family room for lunch when the assistant *gabbai*, Barry Segal, came by after services. "Next *Shabbes* I'll be there," Dad promises Barry, "back on the job." "Good, we'll expect you," Barry beams. Two days later Dad's gone.

The 911 responders carefully dry his body, place it on a white bedsheet, lift and position it on his side of Mom and Dad's bed, and leave. I call a few people to let them know Dad's died. Mom stays with Dad. He's still warm, she keeps pointing out, like he could wake up at any time.

I start making calls about funeral arrangements. There's a problem with people staying with the body, as is traditional, between the *taharah* (the ritual washing and dressing of the body) and the funeral service and burial. The funeral home can do a *taharah,* but they lock the place for the night for security, so anyone staying with the body would have to be locked inside the entire night. They can get a "professional" to stay with the body. That's not what we want. We want friends to be able to do this, the way we've been doing in Durham/Chapel Hill for generations. People take 2 hour shifts, often for close to 24 hours.

The only solution we can work out in Pasadena/Los Angeles is for the funeral home to bring Dad's body back to our home after the *taharah* where we can have people, *shomrim* (guards), stay with his body until the funeral service and burial. Because some people are coming from across the country for the funeral, we decide to delay it until Wednesday. So we need *shomrim* for almost 48 hours. People from PJTC, the Pasadena Temple, I think Edie Taylor, generously organize this. A pair of Chassidic men come to get Dad's body that afternoon. They are very respectful, appropriate.

As their hearse leaves the house, Mom keeps reciting the priestly blessing *Y'vorechecho Adonai V'yismorecho....* I think she has special affinity toward this prayer, being a *Bas Kohen*, daughter of a *Kohen*, the priestly caste. The men drive the hearse away very slowly, at a funereal pace, for the full two long blocks of Loma Vista Street, until they reach its end and have to turn on Altadena Drive.

That evening, another pair of Chassids drive back with Dad's body in a plain coffin now. One of them introduces himself. He grew up at PJTC, not very religious at the time, but says he wanted to do this *mitzvah* of participating in Dad's *taharah* and driving him back because he had such fond memories of Dad's leadership in services at PJTC. It's very touching how many people have been touched by Dad's devotion over the decades he was *gabbai.*

We have cleared my old room to serve as the place where Dad's coffin can stay during the next two days and nights. It has a separate entrance, so the various *shomrim* can come and go easily, even in the middle of the night. We're told that so many people have called to sign up that there were no more times available, and that they started allowing multiple people to sign up for each time slot. Indeed, people quietly come and go from the room.

Marta arrives early and was in the room with someone the first evening when Melanie arrives with Sam and Miriam. Marta offers to leave to allow Melanie and the children some private time with Dad, but Melanie says, no, you're welcome to stay. Sam has already started to prepare for his Bar Mitzvah which is less than 2 years away, and he softly recites a portion of the prayers next to Dad's coffin.

People continue to come and go quietly. I wake during the night and go sit by Dad's coffin. There are several *shomrim* in the room. Very comforting.

The funeral is overflowing with people. I notice Otto Wolman among the honorary pallbearers behind the coffin. Such a good friend to Dad. I remember he gave to Dad a lovely old set of *Five Books of Moses* with the Wolman name in it and his dedication to Dad underneath. I remember thinking that since he was older than Dad, that this was his way of passing on this set of holy books to the next generation. *Oy.* Not to be.

It was good that Edie Taylor had realized before the funeral that there would be too many people at the *shiva minyan* that evening to fit into our house, so she arranged for the *minyan* to be at the temple. Good thinking, indeed, since the number of people almost filled up the entire sanctuary.

Even the *shiva minyans* on subsequent evenings were too big for our house. The overflow of people spilled out onto the front porch and further out onto the front lawn. All these people to honor such a humble individual, Dad, who genuinely didn't think of himself as anyone special. Many years ago, when he heard that he was selected as PJTC Congregant of the Year, his first reaction was, "This must be some mistake. Surely they must mean somebody else."

A *Lamedvavnik*.

There's a Hassidic tradition that there are always 36 (*lamed-vav*) hidden righteous people in the world to justify the world's existence. They don't even know themselves that they are one. When one of them dies, their role is assumed, unknowingly, by another.

Who now to replace Dad?

Marta

Two young Chassids in black, wearing white shirts and black hats, brought Dad home late that Monday evening in March of 2000. Dad had collapsed and died in the morning while taking his daily shower. The caregiver screamed, my brother and mother came running. Dad lay in a heap, lifeless, on the floor of the shower stall. I was deeply saddened I couldn't be there with him, having left only a few days prior.

They say the Good are rewarded by a quick and painless passing. If anyone earned that, Dad certainly had.

Waiting at the airport a few hours later, I watched a father playing with his young daughter, completely delighting in one another. He looked European and appeared to be just a few years younger than Dad would have been when I was the little girl's age. After we landed I saw them again at baggage claim. They were so natural and happy being together. I couldn't resist commenting.

"It's wonderful to see how you are with your daughter." "Why?" He looked puzzled, as if asking what's so special about it? "It reminds me of how my Dad was with me, and I am so grateful. He just passed away this morning. Your daughter is going to feel grateful too, when she's my age, for having had such a kind father." "Thank you" he said, took his daughter's hand and walked on.

The Chassids, Moishe the young one, the other middle-aged, drove from the Los Angeles mortuary in a plain white delivery van. They pulled up the driveway to the rear of the house next to the back door to Henry's old bedroom we had quickly cleared out for Dad. They were men with a simple, solid presence, men of apparent dignity, devotion, compassion, and vitality. Dad would have liked and admired them. The older one, Bruce Bloom, had prepared Dad and remembered him fondly from the '60s growing up in the Pasadena Temple even though his family moved away upon his high school graduation in 1967. When he heard Dad had died and that they would be doing *tahara*, the ritual cleansing and purifying of the body, he knew he wanted not only to prepare Dad but also personally bring him home to us.

As Mom, Henry, and I watched solemnly, they carried in the casket, a simple pine box, just what Dad had requested. A beautiful *Mogen David* with a circle around it was carved on top. I hoped Dad wouldn't mind, considering it too fancy. The Star of David was draped with the *tzitzes* that had been cut from one of the four corners of his *tallis*, rendering his prayer shawl no longer useable and Dad no longer bound by the religious responsibility of the living. Dad's large traditional black and white *tallis* he used most of his life was forever wrapped around him now.

"You can keep it," Mom softly offered as we gazed upon the *tzitzes*, striking tangible proof that Dad was no longer with us. "Your brother already has your father's *tfillin*." Years before, Henry and Dad had exchanged theirs, as Dad had done with *his* father when he buried him.

I have those *tzitzes* in my bedroom now, on a little table with his white satin *yarmulke* he wore at home every *Shabbes.* He asked me to embroider this *yarmulke* when he first got it, the design my choice, the color his, maroon. I chose a flowing pattern, echoing ocean waves, that I stitched along the rim. It always made me happy to see him joyfully wear it, and it makes me happy each time I see it now. His glasses and a photo of him are on the table, too. It's the photo our friend Kathy Kobayashi took of him standing under his lemon tree holding a Torah adorned with a crown made from fresh flowers minutes before by my mother and temple folks, a tradition of my mother's family in Kistokaj in honor of Shavuos.

"Did you enclose a spoon?" I asked Bruce, the older Chassid. "No," he looked at me quizzically. "My father told us that when the Messiah comes and brings everyone back to life, they can dig their way out with it." I went to the kitchen and picked a spoon used for milk, not meat, being the vegetarian in the family. I smiled thinking that I used to joke with Dad that if the Messiah had the power to resurrect people, why would they need spoons?

"Could I take one last look at him?" I asked, standing behind Bruce as he lifted the top to place the spoon next to Dad's hand. Silently he closed the lid, gently held my arm, took me aside, and kindly looked at me. "As you know, we don't use any embalming, and your father was quickly deteriorating because of his condition. His face has already caved in. I want you to remember him as you do, not like he is now." Indeed, my father at nearly 89 had outlived his medical condition and the experience of all his doctors. "He is living from sheer joy and the will to live," they all had said.

As the Chassids left, walking backwards out of the room in symbolic gesture of reluctance in the face of death, I started the first shift at midnight of the informal *Chevra*

Kadisha we created to honor my father who had always spoken about his sacred role in the *Chevra Kadisha* in Tokaj. I remember Dad saying that one of the things he did was step down into the graves to close the eyes of the departed, often needing to put a piece of pottery on their eyes to keep them shut.

Friends and family came continuously around the clock to sit with Dad, silently reading from the Book of Psalms according to Jewish tradition, until he was taken for Wednesday morning's funeral. Pure and simple love emanated from that room as my father lay alongside the tall *shiva* candle encased in a beautiful blue glass, the light flickering on the photographs I placed near him. In every picture, Dad is beaming in the company of those he loved so much.

The next night, my brother's family arrived from across the country, and my nephew Sam came right in. Standing next to Dad he began chanting the introductory blessing to his Haftorah. He wanted Grandpa to hear how he had already been practicing for his Bar Mitzvah a year and a half away.

Over 200 people filled the old mortuary chapel. Dozens were standing against the walls. My father, a simple, working class, salt of the earth *tzadik,* had become everyone's father and grandfather, their link to the Old Country, their *gabbai* for over 30 years. My brother and I sat behind the privacy curtains, comforting our mother, waiting for our kids and spouses to arrive. It was getting later and later. They must be caught in LA traffic. "Don't worry, my dear," I heard my father gently say to me in Hungarian as I glanced over at his casket. "I'm not going anywhere." Calmly, I started silently singing *Shalom Aleichem* and heard my father's melodious voice high above mine. We were singing just like we had done every *Shabbes,* welcoming the separation of the hard work week from the restful and joyful Sabbath my father in his clean white shirt always looked forward to.

After a few of us spoke warmly about Dad, I read out loud the letters to the kids he had dictated to me in the hospital. Prayers were recited and the time had come to bury him.

I followed Mom and Henry up the aisle behind Dad, his casket carried by three pairs of fathers and sons including my own, through the throngs of devoted friends and family, all grieving and honoring this man we all loved so much. I hurried to catch up and be closer to him but also held back, not wanting to let him go.

At the gravesite, as I watched others ritually scatter dirt over him, I couldn't stop squeezing my son's hand. Burning tears welled up in my eyes and flowed down my face. Suddenly, a serene sense of joy washed over me as I thought just how fitting this is: Dad is being planted into the rich and fertile earth just like he loved to plant and care for the flowers and fruit trees in his magnificent garden.

May his soul rise to the heavens like the blades of grass around us, and may his memory be a blessing for us all.

20

Visiting the Kubinyis

Left to right: Emese and Anna Kubinyi, Zoltán Kubinyi's great grandchildren; Sam, Sophie, Miriam, Jacob; Márton and Mónika Kubinyi
Back row: Marta and Henry

In June 2011, the day before what would have been Dad's 100th birthday, we went to visit the Kubinyis. Henry and I had not seen Zoltán Kubinyi's son Márton and his wife Mónika since we met them in 1994 at the Holocaust Commemoration in Tokaj when I spoke about his father. We now wanted our children to finally meet them, too, since they had heard so much about their Grandpa's rescuer.

The six of us arrived in their small town, about an hour and a half west of Tokaj, with great anticipation. As we're parking across the street, Márton and Mónika are waving and coming out to meet us. Two teenage girls, their granddaughters, are with them. We excitedly greet each other as everyone is introduced and embraces. It feels just like visiting family.

No sooner do we sit down in the living room than Mónika brings from the kitchen a feast. Drinks and lunch plus a myriad of pastries she's baked, all simply beautiful and delicious. The kids, whose eyes have grown considerably while admiring the pastries, say *köszönöm*, thank you, with wide smiles, and the Kubinyis are clearly delighted that the kids know a bit of Hungarian. We talk about what everyone is doing and I wonder when it might be appropriate to start talking about the person that brought us all together.

"I have a little gift for you." I take a little scrapbook out of my bag and hand it to Márton. It's a little album of photos I had taken in Jerusalem in 2005 in the Garden of the Righteous at Yad Vashem. After searching for hours among beautiful trees and garden paths, I finally found the wall that has his father's name inscribed along with others who had been honored for rescuing Jews during the Holocaust.

I point to the photo showing four stones on top of the wall. "Since I felt that this was, in essence, your father's resting place, I wanted to put a stone on it as is Jewish custom at gravesites. I decided to put one stone for each of my father's four grandchildren, and said *Kaddish*, the mourner's prayer, in appreciation and sorrow." Tears well up in Mónika's eyes and mine and Márton is visibly moved as well.

Garden of the Righteous, Yad Vashem
Jerusalem, 2005

4 stones placed in memory of Zoltán Kubinyi
on top of the wall that bears his name

Garden of the Righteous, Yad Vashem
Jerusalem, 2005

Following the photos, I included a copy of my article, "Sharing a Legacy of Rescue," about his father and meeting them in 1994. As I was translating key sections, they said that Dad had sent one of the published versions of the article, but it didn't have any of the photos we were now enjoying together: Dad in his late 20's before the war; his father before the war, 10 years older than Dad; Mom and Dad in 1996 at 50 years of marriage; his parents in 1942 on the occasion of their engagement. Lives fully lived despite war, others cut short and ruined because of it.

Dad and Mom, married 50 years

Pasadena, 1996

Jacob
my son

Visiting the Kubinyis held the same feeling for me as visiting distant family. Excitement, anticipation, warmth, and welcoming. Although we may live very far away from each other, there is a strange comfort and familiarity that persists purely by virtue of what feels like a familial connection. Even stranger is to have this feeling without being able to communicate in the same language.

Upon arriving at the Kubinyis' house, a full day of animated pantomimes and lightning-speed translations commenced. Our two families sharing a strong common bond, yet only a vague personal relationship. Four speak only Hungarian, four only English, and two succeeding to engage and translate simultaneously!

We chatted about all of our own lives and endeavors for a little while, then transitioned to talking about the two men who made this experience happen: Zoltán and Grandpa. If not for the courage of Zoltán, our family would not be here. His family was forced to grow up without a father. Our family had a father because of him.

Sophie
my daughter

As the morning came when we were going to drive and meet the son of Zoltán Kubinyi, a man I have only heard about through conversations and readings, I couldn't help but develop a swarm of feelings and thoughts. The first thing that I thought about was how I wished Grandpa were driving with us to experience this moment and share with Kubinyi's son the memories and feelings he had about his father. Instead, only we could express ourselves to this man and share with him how we feel and how we think Grandpa felt.

When we approached the house, a lovely old woman came out and greeted us happily, followed by her husband, the younger but older looking Kubinyi. The first thing I felt when they hugged us and gave us traditional Hungarian kisses was a feeling of family. I have never met them before, I never met or knew the man who saved Grandpa, but after hearing the stories I felt like I was meeting family members.

Once inside, I got excited to hear what they had to say, even if I couldn't understand anything in Hungarian and needed translation. To see their body movements and personality interested me enough. I didn't have to know what they were saying but just witness their image. I felt like I was taking mental pictures to show later to Grandpa. "When you have some time, Grandpa, I want to show you pictures of the Kubinyis."

As I watched everyone interact and listened to my uncle translate the words, I could see how interested everyone was in listening to stories. My mom and uncle were interested in hearing what the son had to say about his father and the stories he knew about. Mr. Kubinyi and his wife were interested to know what we had to say about his father and how grateful we felt for Grandpa being saved. All I could think was had his father, a brave and wonderful man, not saved my Grandpa, none of us would be here.

The entire time being with these lovely people made such an impact on everyone. To be close to the real rescuer is amazing. You sit with his family and you feel a presence of him himself. I only wish I could have witnessed a conversation between the rescuer Kubinyi and my survivor Grandpa. I imagine, though, that both were present in the room with us all and admiring everything and everyone just as we were.

21

Memories of Grandpa

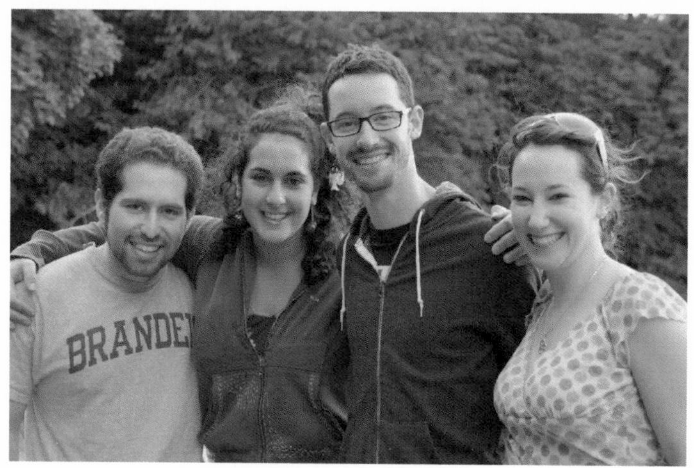

Sam, Miriam, Jacob, Sophie

Tokaj, Summer 2011

Sam
Henry's son

I remember watering the garden -- the flowers and all the fruit trees – with *Nagypapa* whenever we went to visit. I also remember always giving him a big hug whenever we first arrived at the house after getting in at the airport. We would usually go around through the back door, and the table was already set and *Nagymama* and *Nagypapa* were doing final preparations.

I've been reflecting a lot over the past few weeks since

graduating from college, and I keep thinking how proud *Nagypapa* (as well as my *Bubbe*, my mother's mom) would be of me and catch myself thinking at times "if they could see me now." I like to think in some way they can. I was one of the supervisors/coordinators for the Brandeis Reunion this past weekend, and at the final event (a jazz brunch) the new president spoke to the alums about how returning to Brandeis (and supporting it) is about being connected to something larger than yourself. I started to tear up not just because of President Lawrence's words, but because ten minutes before I walked by and said hello to him because we've spoken several times and he knows who I am. After that was when I was thinking "I hope you can see me now".

I also love that I have *Nagypapa's yarmulke*, the large colorful, embroidered one that's like a small hat. I keep it in my *tallis* bag, and while I do not wear it that often I remember putting it on during the recent High Holidays. I also love that on my Bar Mitzvah *Nagymama* gave me one of his prayer books, and on my graduation she gave me two other books of his.

I still feel very connected to *Nagypapa*. He went through so much and left his home so his children could have more opportunities, and did everything needed to ensure they would thrive (and they have). My dad tells me he always sent money to him during college (not necessarily a lot, but would send it frequently) even though my dad didn't think he needed it. He just told him he should be ok while he was studying, because education was important (At least I think that's how he phrased it to Henry). When I was going through old papers in my room at Chapel Hill, I found the letter I received from Cary Academy, my middle and high school, saying I would be attending school there, and on the top is a fax sticky note that I used when I faxed it to *Nagymama* and *Nagypapa* (at my father's suggestion). He knew I was going to a good school, and while I cannot remember if he said anything to me about the next time I saw him, I like to think he was happy and proud of me when he found out.

Miriam
Henry's daughter

Some of my favorite memories of *Nagypapa* were during the early mornings we would spend together in Pasadena. Every time we would visit, I would try to wake up before *Nagypapa*. I would tiptoe out into the kitchen, hoping that I had finally woken up first. Yet every single morning, he would be sitting in his white leather armchair, reading the paper. Once he saw me, he would just smile, and hand me the comics.

After we finished reading, we would walk out into the orchard and pick the best looking oranges and tangerines we could find in order to make freshly squeezed orange juice for the family. We would pull out the juicer and make as much orange juice as we could. At this point I was still too short to reach the kitchen counter properly, so I had to use that stepping stool that was always sitting by the cellar door in order to reach the juicer.

As the morning went on, more of the family woke up and would "test" our juice to make sure it was good enough (it always was). I loved spending mornings with *Nagypapa*, reading and making orange juice, because they were our special time together.

Jacob
my son

Grandpa really enjoyed playing chess with all of his grandchildren. I played with him often, and somehow, no matter how young I was, I always managed to beat him. Of course, Grandpa simply let me win every time. But at the moment I would tip over his King, he would go into a joking chant of "That's not fair! That's not fair!" pounding his fist on the table to prove he had really tried to beat me. The only thing that gave him away was his huge smile.

*

I will always remember Grandpa's wonderful sense of humor. He had a particular sense of irony, poking fun at silly situations with much endearment. One of his favorite jokes, which I heard several times as a kid, went like this:

Grandpa: "What's the difference between a car seat and pin?"

Me: "What...?"

Grandpa: "Sit on them and you'll find out!!"

He would tell this short and sweet joke with a huge grin on his face, and a good chuckle afterwards.

*

I remember every year when I was very little, we would visit Grandma and Grandpa for New Year's. This was especially exciting because of the Rose Parade and how close the house was to the parade itself. Even though we always planned to get up early and camp out on the street to catch the end of the parade in person, I remember getting up extra early each New Year's morning to watch all the excitement on TV in bed with Grandma and Grandpa. These early mornings with Grandma and Grandpa were even more fun than being at the actual parade!

*

One memory that sticks with me relates to Grandpa's final letter to me before he passed away. I was sixteen at the time and just learning to drive. He mentions in the letter that I should learn all the traffic rules and drive safely.

When I was a little kid, perhaps 8 years old, we went to Disneyland. This was not my first time there, so I knew what rides I wanted to go on. One of my favorites was Mr. Toad's Wild Ride, one that takes you in a car haphazardly through the story of The Wind and the Willows. Well since I had been on this ride before, I knew that the driver's seat was the place to be. Of course Grandpa let me have that seat, fake spinning turning wheel and all. We went through the ride and had a blast.

As we were exiting, Grandpa shakes his head and tells me that after such terrible driving he would never let me drive again!! Not until I proved that I could drive better than that! I found this to be hilarious, and it became an on-going joke with us.

Sophie
my daughter

I remember when my Grandpa died I couldn't help but wonder what it meant to me. He was gone and I was young and never experienced someone so close to me leaving my side. How was I supposed to react? I didn't know the answer. I wondered why it had to happen. If they're someone everyone loves and respects and wants around in their world, how can they just disappear? Why must they disappear? Back then I wasn't sure what the answers to my questions would be. Now that I am much older, I think more about it and have come to some conclusions.

My Grandpa was someone I loved. He was a man that created great memories for me to have with me now. He physically disappeared but emotionally is always here with me and my family and all his friends. His body crumbled, a body that was only a container for the man. Everything that made up my Grandpa, everything that helped to create the man he was, will always be with me. His spirit and life will remain in the world and we will tell his stories and ours about him.

*

I remember in Pasadena one day, it was just me and Grandpa alone in the house while everyone else was out. We watched "I Love Lucy" together, laughing until it was over. Grandpa then wanted me to find us something else to watch (I was in charge of the remote), so I flipped the channels and found a perfect show, "Leave It To Beaver."

Grandpa fell asleep and snored a few times which made me softly giggle. About an hour later he woke up and smiled at me saying, "*Jaj*, Sophieka. I fell asleep?" I nodded yes, smiling, thinking how peaceful he looked when sleeping. Grandpa looked at me with his loving face, realizing I had been in the room the whole time, watching TV as he napped, never once waking him up. Then Grandpa got up out of his chair and walked over to the kitchen and offered me something to eat. We had a little snack and watched another "Leave It To Beaver" until the rest of the family came home.

*

Every young child has their favorite game to play. They have the game they will always enjoy playing as they grow up, the game they want to teach their own kids when they are little, and then the games they will continue playing not because they love it but because it reminds them of memories. For me, my memory game is chess.

Chess was never my favorite game to play as a young girl because it was hard and required lots and lots of concentration and strategy. However, it is a game that will always be a part of me because it was the game every grandchild would play with our Grandpa.

One day, when Grandpa was visiting us, he and I sat down at the dining room table to play a nice game of chess. Grandpa was always very good at the game, whereas I was always trying but still never achieving the right moves. To Grandpa, winning or losing was never his goal. His goal was to teach me, for me to learn, and for us to spend some time together.

As the game progressed, I was losing, but every move I made I was learning something. "If I move the bishop here instead, that blocks him there." Grandpa sees that I am learning based on his teaching and even though at the end of the game I lost, Grandpa was proud of me. He smiled up at me and said, "Good game, Sophieka" and shook my hand. We weren't opponents, we were granddaughter and grandfather.

*

Although I never got a huge joy out of attending synagogue, I managed to have my little moments of happiness watching my Grandpa, the *gabbai,* on the *bima* calling people up to the Torah. To listen to him chant Hebrew and gaze at me in the congregation always put a smile on my face. I never fully understood the words he would be saying in Hebrew, but it didn't matter to me because this was my Grandpa, a man who was proud and comfortable being a Hungarian Jew.

As I watch my Grandpa and see him smile at me and my family in the congregation, I am filled with happiness. Who knew temple could be tolerable after all? As the Torah service comes to an end, Grandpa walks off the *bima* and takes a seat on the bench in front of me, his *tallis* flowing down over the wooden bench. He opens his prayer book and then turns his head and winks at me. Every time that wink came I knew how happy Grandpa was to see me, his grandchild, in synagogue with him.

The service continues for some time and I am beginning to fade and want to take a snooze. It turns out I was not the only one, as I noticed Grandpa nodding off as well. I smiled and giggled to my mom as I watched Grandpa in front of me. Luckily, soon after, the service concluded and we stood up and wished each other a good *Shabbes.* Grandpa approached me and hugged me and kissed me on the cheeks, whispering "Good *Shabbes*, Sophieka."

*

My favorite memory of Grandpa and me is the famous 4 kisses story. Every visit, Grandpa would pick us up and drop us off at the airport. He smiled at all of us and gave each of us hugs and kisses with much love. “Mártika! How wonderful it is to see you” as he wraps his arms around my mom. “Jacobka! How are you? I’ve missed you!” And finally, as I’m standing next to everyone and watching Grandpa embrace my mom and brother, he finally turns to me. “Sophieka! How many kisses?” “Four!” I answer enthusiastically, and Grandpa would kiss me on my cheeks, 2 on one, 2 on the other. Each visit I was asked the same question and always replied with the same answer, four.

Then one day, Grandpa asked, “Sophieka, how many kisses today?” I thought for a moment and replied, “Three!” Grandpa looks at me with his warm twinkle in the eye, smiles, and then says, “That’s not enough!” as he begins to give me lots more.

Every time I relive that story I smile. My Grandpa was a good Grandpa who loved everyone so much and wasn’t afraid to show it.

22

The Tokaj Jewish Cemetery

The plum trees are no longer there in the old Jewish cemetery. They were the same flourishing trees that filled our garden in Tokaj, producing delicious plums I remember Mom once giving basketfuls of to a lady in exchange for tickets to the circus that had come to town. When Henry and I last visited the cemetery with Dad -- twenty years ago it now has been -- the plums were ripe and tempting. As I was about to reach for one, Dad gently said that it wasn't appropriate to eat fruit that's growing in a cemetery. I don't really know why. It wasn't important to ask.

The old gravestones are so worn that the Hebrew is barely readable, but they are upright and mostly intact because they have been taken care of by our childhood friends Lajcsi and Miki. Lajcsi with a group of volunteers, young students from other countries, marked and photographed the tombstones. Lajcsi and Miki have also overseen the tradition of retaining a caretaker who lives in the house next to the cemetery, his lodging provided in exchange for work needed to preserve the past and honor the people resting here.

Lajcsi suddenly passed away the week before our visit in the summer of 2011. Henry was in Barcelona at a conference when he heard the shocking news. He managed to make it to the funeral held the next day, quickly flying to Budapest and driving down to Tokaj with Öcsi, another childhood friend who will now help Miki with the cemetery.

I came the following week with our children. How odd it was to see the grave of our contemporary, buried next to his parents, in the cemetery he cared for with such dedication. When I said goodbye to him on our last visit, I told him how much we appreciate all that he does. "Lajcsi, you're the *Ner Tamid,* the Eternal Light, of the Tokaj Jewish Community." He was visibly moved.

Lajos (Lajcsi) Löwy

Tokaj Jewish Cemetery
2008

Whenever I'm here in this beautiful, old and peaceful cemetery, it feels like coming home. Members of both sides of our family are buried here, those who had the chance to live and die according to the natural order of life and death. Henry once pointed to the field of empty space off to the side. Yes, I nodded, sacred land meant for family and friends who were brutally taken and unceremoniously discarded, their absence visibly apparent and palpably felt here and elsewhere in town.

We visit the graves of Mom's relatives and Dad's parents and say the traditional prayers. Dad's parents were fortunate to die before the deluge of Holocaust destruction, unlike Mom's parents who Mengele at Auschwitz decided we would never know.

symbolic stones we placed on a gravesite in Tokaj cemetery, 2011

Standing at the grave of Dad's mother, I recalled what he told me about how she died in 1935 at 64 years of age when he was 24. She died on January 20th, the same day Henry was born 13 years later. Dad was over at the Liebermans listening to the radio when suddenly the servant girl came and said his mother was sick and that he should come right away. He found her in bed having difficulty breathing. He went to get Dr. Sándor Moskovitz who lived near where our music teacher Irénke *néni* lived. He was in bed, already sleep. Dad ran home, the doctor came ten minutes later. He examined his mother and said she had died.

Dad contacted the head of the *Chevra Kadisha,* Rosenberg, who was Gyula Wassermann's oldest sister's husband, and he came over with some straw and laid it on the floor onto which he laid Dad's mother, covering her with a white sheet. He lit a long, 12 inch white candle that burned the entire night while Dad and his father sat with her all night. In the morning, Dad notified his brother Volvi, not wanting to disturb him and his family late at night.

The next day, the clerk of the *Chevra Kadisha* went to the Temple, and then door to door, with the *pushkeh*, the collection box, saying in Yiddish, "Charity saves your life, charity saves you from death." Everyone asked who died and when will the funeral be, and gave something. This is what enabled the *Chevra Kadisha* to maintain its services.

An old Jewish man brought wood to the house and family and friends took turns making the casket, as was the tradition, measuring the body with a string. White material was also brought, and by hand people took turns sewing the dress. It had no pockets, symbolizing that you leave this world the same as you entered it, taking nothing.

Dad's mother, Ida Billitzer

Tokaj, 1897

Painting by Pál Gyoroki

From a small photograph that was probably her wedding portrait taken when she was 24 or 25 years old

Dad's father died in 1940 at age 76 when Dad was 29 and already in labor camp. He died the day after Shavuos, the same day his grandfather Yitschak Isaac Billitzer, the esteemed rabbi of Nagy Ida, had died.

I remembered Dad proudly telling me what the rabbi had said in his eulogy: "When a man dies and goes before God, the first question God will ask him is, 'Did you conduct your business affairs honestly?' And the rabbi said that Y'Heschel Fuchs will be able to proudly say, 'Yes, my Lord, I engaged in business honestly.'"

I also recalled Dad telling me about the last time he saw his father, two months before his death, and how he thought that maybe his father already knew he was going to die. Dad and his brother Vilmos (Volvi) were called up for labor camp, and their father accompanied them out in a fiacre along with Volvi's wife and kids.

Dad said that when they parted and he looked back, he saw his father bent over with his hands on his face crying. Dad thought maybe his father knew this would be the last time he'd see his brother Volvi and him. And it was.

Top right corner:

Signature of Dad's father, Henrik Fuchs

Tokaj, 1909
City Hall records

No photograph remains of him
Perhaps none was ever taken, Dad thought

Like Dad used to do, I tore some grass from the earth and put them on his parents' tombstones, placing little stones on top to secure them. The stones are all that people place symbolically these days. "Why the grass?" I once asked Dad. "So that their souls will rise up. And when the Messiah comes, according to the old Jewish belief, their life will continue like grass that is torn but not pulled, and they will live on in Israel. The modern Jewish interpretation is that it is in the memory of their children and grandchildren and all those who love them that they will live on."

Sophie
my daughter

As soon as my shoes touched the cobblestones of Tokaj I couldn't help but feel a strong connection to my heritage. To be walking on the ground that my mom walked on when she was a little girl and the ground that my Grandpa walked around on for years, to breathe in the Hungarian air, eat the Hungarian food, and drink the Hungarian water, it all makes me feel so close to family.

I remember walking by the little Tokaj Museum where Grandpa's store used to be, and smiling, thinking I could just walk in and greet my Grandpa with a huge smile and hug. But then reality sunk in and I realized that now it's only in my dreams that I can walk into the building and see an old Hungarian Jew. Not just my Grandpa but any Hungarian Jew of my Grandpa's generation. To know that there are only a few Jews left in Tokaj makes me sad.

While standing outside the beautiful new Synagogue with the twinkling sunlight shining through the Stars of David on me, I think about how powerful that moment would be to Grandpa. When I first saw that majestic building, I stood in awe gazing upon each individual sign of Judaism. I sensed Grandpa standing next to me gazing upon it as well, but not just at the Synagogue but also on me, his grown granddaughter soaking in her heritage of being a Hungarian Jew. I imagine he would tear up watching me embrace the moment. As I stood back taking some photos, I could hear Grandpa's voice through the wind blowing on my face.

Walking back to the main square, I heard Grandpa's footsteps next to mine. I heard him telling me stories about life for him in Tokaj. His voice was with me all through Tokaj, and I felt him holding my hand as we walked into the Tokaj Cemetery in the evening. The trees were filled with many shades of green, the sky was beginning to turn bright colors, and Grandpa led me to the gravesite of his parents.

I stood in the grass staring quietly at the graves and heard myself ask Grandpa about his parents and what he remembers about them. “Grandpa, what were they like? Do you think they would have wanted to know me?” I saw through the wind blowing in the trees my Grandpa in tears, soaking in the moment with me. I could hear him say, “Of course, Sophieka! They would have loved you like I do.” And then he would smile and embrace me in his arms.

As I stood for a while by the tombstones of Grandpa's parents with Grandpa by my side, I turned around for a moment and looked at the sunset with still a few colors left in the sky. "Beautiful, just like you, Sophieka," I heard Grandpa whisper to me. I smiled and turned back to face the tombstones. I squeezed Grandpa's hand and said *Kaddish* for his parents before heading down the little hill to exit the cemetery.

As the gate closed, I felt Grandpa leaving my side. "Go ahead, Sophieka, I need to rest now. I'll see you soon."

"*Jó északát*, good night, Grandpa," I heard myself say, and I walked away from the cemetery thinking how Grandpa is resting with his mother and father tonight in Tokaj.

*

I can't imagine never knowing such a wonderful man as Grandpa. And I can't help but think a lot about Zoltán Kubinyi, the man who rescued my Grandpa. I've only known this man through stories and already he feels like part of the family.

I can't help but think that if this *mensch* of a man hadn't had an ounce of compassion in his heart, my Grandpa would never have been in my life. My mom wouldn't be here. She wouldn't have had my brother and me. I wouldn't be in this world. The stories everyone is hearing about my Grandpa wouldn't exist had this wonderful man not saved him during a brutal time.

It is amazing to think about one single person making a difference in so many lives.

Epilogue

Dad
Tokaj, 1946

Once when we were talking about his life, I gently turned to Dad and asked, "Why do you think you survived?"

Without a moment's hesitation, he answered, "So that I could have a daughter like you who would tell what happened."

It has been an honor.

Happy 100th Birthday, Dad.

Fuchs and Billitzer Family Histories

Bodrog River, Tokaj, 2011

From *Fragments of a Family: Remembering Hungary, the Holocaust, and Emigration to a New World (p.7-15)* ~

To provide more details of both sides of his family, Dad wrote in Hungarian the following two documents (which I translated):

Fuchs Family History
by Morton (Miksa) Fuchs, June 1984

My name is Morton (Miksa) Fuchs (Mordechay Yehuda ben Yechezkel). I was born in Tokaj, Zemplén county, Hungary on June 30, 1911.

My father's name was Fuchs Henrik (Yechezkel ben Mordechay Yehuda). He was born in 1867 in the town of Mocsonok which in those days was part of Hungary in the county of Nyitra. My father died in 1941, the day after Shavuos, in Tokaj and he was buried there.

My father's father, my grandfather, was Fuchs Miksa (Mordechay Yehuda ben H.R.[3] Binyomen Zev). He died in 1911 in Tokaj and he was buried there.

3 H.R.stands for Ha Rav, meaning Rabbi.

My grandfather's father, my great grandfather, was Fuchs Benjamin (H.R. Binjomen Zev Ben ?—not noted on his gravestone whose son he was.) He was Rabbi in the town of Lovas Berény in Fejer county, Hungary. Later he was elected Chief Rabbi sometime later in Vág-Szered. He died in 1870 and is buried there. After his death, his son Fuchs Mór (H.R. Moshe Hirsh ben Binjomen Zev) inherited his position. Fuchs Mór was born in 1843 in Lovas Berény and at 26 years of age he took his late father's vacant place. In 1882 he was invited to be the Chief Rabbi in Nagyvárad, Bihar county, in Hungary in those days, where until his death in 1911 he served in this capacity. Fuchs Miksa, my grandfather, was his older brother.

After his death, his son, Fuchs Benyamin (H.R. Binjomen ben Moshe Hirs) filled his vacant position of Chief Rabbi until the end of his life. He died in 1936.

My great grandfather, H.R. Fuchs Benjamin, had ten children, two boys and eight girls. The oldest son was Fuchs Miksa who was my grandfather. His other son was Fuchs Mór, the Chief Rabbi of Nagyvárad. His eight sons-in-law were: Ringvald Eizik, Ringvald Volf, Ringvald Naftule Hercz, Grosz Israel, Miller Jichok, Kecskeméti Naftule Hercz, Rubinstein Majer, and Ehrenfeld ? [first name unknown].

The names of the daughters are not listed in the chronicles because in those days the women and girls did not count, and in the old Jewish writings they did not appear unless they distinguished themselves in some extraordinary way.

My grandfather Fuchs Miksa had three sons and I believe several daughters, but I only know about one of them. I don't remember her name. Her husband was Gersohn Stern who was Rabbi in the city of Maros Ludas, Hungary. I knew him well. He came to my parents' house often, when I was 8-10 years old. I remember his warm smile and kindly fine words.

My grandfather's three sons were Fuchs Henrik, my father, of Tokaj; Fuchs Mór who lived in Homona, then also part of Hungary; and Fuchs Vilmos who was the Principal of the Jewish School in Szeged, and the director of the Temple choir there

* *

8

History of one branch of the Billitzer family
by Morton (Miksa) Fuchs , December 1996

For a long time I have considered the thought of writing down the history of my late mother's side of the family, as much as I can remember. I knew the members of our family who perished during the Holocaust or who died before it. The older facts I gathered from the book Bér Jichok, The Well of Yitschak, which was written by one of the members of the Billitzer family, and it is partly about one part of the family's history. Some information I also gathered from the Encyclopedia Judaica, Volume 8, under the name Horovitz.

The original name of the Billitzer family was Horovitz. The oldest date which I found in the books goes back to 1565 in Prague where one of our ancestors was born that year, Isaiah ben Ábraham Hálévi Horovitz. It was a very wealthy family, and they were highly respected Talmud scholars. The young Isaiah had studied at many famous rabbi yeshivas when he was selected at a fairly young age to the Bet-Din, the rabbinical court, for life, in the city of Dubno in Poland. Later he returned to Prague where he served as rabbi until 1621 when he emigrated to Jerusalem in the land of Palestine. In Jerusalem the Ashkenazi community elected him rabbi. He died in Tiberias in the year 1660 and was buried there near the famous Maimonides grave.

One branch of the Horovitz family, Pinches Hálève Horovitz, resided in Germany in the city of Úncdorf where Jichok Eizik ben Pinches Hálévi was born in the year 1801. Some time later, the family, for reasons unknown, wandered to Hungary and took the name of Billitzer. Jichok Eizik ben Pinches Hálevi Billitzer was my great grandfather. His son, Ire Lipman Hálévi Billitzer, was my grandfather. My grandmother's name was Chane. The history books don't talk about her, but I know that she came from a family with the name of Baruch.

My grandfather, Ire Lipman Hálévi Billitzer, was rabbi in Szepesófalu. They had seven children, six girls and one boy.

The oldest daughter was Aunt Róza. Her husband was Adolf Schaffer. They lived in Sátoraljaújhely, Hungary. They had no children. My uncle was a leather merchant and had a store with a partner. Later he made a living in buying and selling produce. When they got old and were no longer capable of working, they took a young Jewish couple to live with them who took care of their needs. At the end of the 1930's, they died within two to three years of each other. My uncle was a *highly respected, very religious man and a great Talmud scholar. They attained a nice old age, and after their death the young couple inherited their house and all of their belongings.*

The second daughter was Aunt Rezsi. She was an angel from heaven. Her husband was Uncle Samu, Samuel Lieberman. He was an exceptionally ambitious, hard-working man. He was the director of the Jewish elementary school in Tokaj. He was the manager of the Tokaj branch of the Borsod Miskolc Credit Bank. He was the editor-in -chief of the Tokaj and Province weekly newspaper. He also maintained a private higher elementary school where he taught every day. In addition, he also had time to be involved in the Jewish Community matters. For a time, he was even the President of the Jewish Community. When he retired, he founded the Association of National Hungarian Businessmen (Országos Magyar Kereskedök Egyesületét, OMKE) and was the President of it until he died. Shopkeepers and craftsmen were its members. The OMKE was open every night. Men gathered together, they played cards and billiards, read newspapers, or talked. They held meetings and conventions, and often there also were dances. Uncle Samu died in 1938. He was diabetic and also had prostate problems. Aunt Rezsi died in 1940. I remember that she suffered a lot in the last years because she felt a ringing in her head continuously, which could not be treated. They had five children, three boys and two girls: Sárika, Erzsike, Ernö, Lajos (Luci), and Gyula.

Sárika — her husband was Artur Novák, a high positioned railway employee. They lived in the city of Ózd. Later they were transferred to the city of Eger. They were deported in 1944 and they didn't come back. They had three children, two girls and one boy: Magda, Kati, and Imre.

Magda — the oldest, was newly married and pregnant when they deported her in 1944, and she didn't come back. Her husband, Dr. Imre Englender, perished as a labor battalion worker.

Kati — her husband was Gyula Propper. They lived in Tolcsva. He was a wine grower. During the time of deportation they escaped to Budapest. The nyilas [Hungarian nazis, the Arrow Cross] captured him and deported him. Kati, with the baby Elizabeth, lived through the war years in a "safe" house until liberation. After the liberation of Budapest she returned to Tolcsva. Gyula also survived the concentration camps and returned to Tolcsva and continued the wine growing and wine selling. In March 1949 they too left the country and emigrated to Canada. They settled in Toronto. Like everyone, they too worked hard for a living. Many years later Gyula died and Kati married again. Her husband, Tibor Lukás, is a retired businessman. Kati has one daughter, Elizabeth, and one son, János. They also live in Toronto. Tibor has one daughter, likewise in Toronto. A doctor is her husband.

Imre — was a labor battalion worker amidst terrible conditions. When his squadron made it up to Budapest after a lot of wandering, he escaped and hid in Budapest. During the siege of Budapest shorty before liberation he was injured and ended up in the hospital. After liberation he learned that his sister Kati had hid in Budapest during the war, and he later re-united with her. For a period of time they were together. Afterwards, Kati went down to Tolcsva with the baby. Imre, after he regained his strength somewhat, went down to Eger. There he relapsed and ended up in the hospital again. He was in the hospital for some weeks. When he recovered completely, he went down to Kati in Tolcsva. He was in Tolcsva for about a year. Then he went up to Budapest and resumed his studies at the Budapest Technical University where he received his engineering diploma. In 1949, with the Zionist movement a chance opened to illegally emigrate to Israel, and after a second attempt, with adventurous circumstances indeed, he succeeded. In Israel he first worked in road construction, with his own truck carried water and building materials. Later then in Beer-Sheva he worked as an engineer in a big chemical factory. His wife, Incike, was from Hajduszoboszló. Incike emigrated on the same boat, at the same time, as Imre, but they only became acquainted in Israel. They have three children, two boys and one girl: Cvi, Gád, and Óra. They live near Beer-Sheva in the small town of Omer.

Erzsike — her husband was Dr. Aladár Glück, he was a doctor. They lived in Tiszapolgár. They had a daughter Marika. They were deported and Marika alone came back. She was in Budapest for a time. Then she went out to Canada with a kindertransport. Marika met her husband Joe Goldlust in Canada and they settled in Toronto. Joe, of Polish origin, had also been deported. They have a company in Toronto. They sell and repair vacuum cleaners and other household cleaning appliances. They have three children, one son and two daughters: Robert, Darlene, and Cheryl.

Ernö — Dr. Ernö Loránd, was a lawyer in Tokaj. His wife was Sárika Gutlohn. They had two children, Gabika and Ivánka. They must have been 10-14 years old.

None of them came back.

Lajos — *Lajos Loránd (Luci) and his wife, Ilonka Heller, had a cosmetology laboratory and salon in Budapest. They had one daughter, Évike. Luci was deported. Ilonka was in a "safe" house with Évike, and from there they took Ilonka one day for work, and she never came back. Évike then ended up in an orphanage and was there until Luci came back from the Mauthausen concentration camp. Shortly thereafter, Luci again opened up the cosmetology laboratory and began to work. For years they waited and hoped that Ilonka escaped and would return. Anuska ~~Szegö~~ a trained cosmetologist, became partners in the cosmetology salon and shortly after, Luci took her as his wife. Anuska was so good to Évike, as if she were her real mother. In 1953 Luci died of leukemia. He is buried in Budapest. Évike became acquainted with Robert Verebes. Robi had finished a music academy, he was a violist, and after the Revolution, he got abroad with his orchestra. But before he left, Évike and he got married with the rabbi. Shortly after, Évike succeeded in illegally going out to Vienna where she met Robi. For a time they were in Vienna. Then they emigrated to Canada and settled in Montreal. Robi joined the Montreal Symphony orchestra, and to this day is there in a high position. He also is a Professor at the Montreal University teaching music. Some years after they arrived in Canada, Anuska joined them and with Évike they opened the cosmetology salon. Anuska died some years ago after a long illness. Évike and Robi have one daughter Lucy and a son Tomi.*

Gyula — *Gyula Lórand, was the director of a bank in Tolcsva. His wife, Aranka Propper, was the daughter of a vineyard owner in Tolcsva. They had one daughter, Veronka. They were deported. Gyula perished in the concentration camp. Aranka and Veronka survived and came back. For a while they were in Tolcsva, then they went to Nyiregyháza where Aranka became partners in some store. In 1949, Veronka had the opportunity to illegally go out to Vienna. She met her first husband, a German Jew who had survived Auschwitz, in Enns where he was working for the Joint and with whom she emigrated to America. They settled in San Francisco. Meanwhile, Aranka remarried a Budapest doctor, Dr. Lajos Nemes, and she moved up to Budapest. Veronka's husband had wanted to go to medical school, but since they had two small children, Évike and Edward, he had to work. He couldn't adapt to life in America, so they separated and he went back to Germany.[4] Veronka remained alone with the children. For years she worked very hard as a registered nurse. She raised the children and educated them. In 1968 she married Marc Berk, a physician, and he passed away in 1994. Meanwhile, Évike and Edward had married, and they made very nice careers. Veronka had changed to*

[4] After 43 years, Veronica contacted him in Berlin, "to let him know that the children have turned out to be decent, successful human beings. He is now in touch with the family."

selling real estate, and in a few short years she became very successful. Aranka often visited Veronka in America. Aranka's husband, Lajos bácsi, died in the beginning of the 1980's. Aranka died in the fall of 1994 in Budapest.

The third Billitzer girl was Ida — she was my mother. My father, Henrik Fuchs, had a grocery store in Tokaj, a salt storehouse, and a flour consignment warehouse. My mother died in January of 1936. My father died in June of 1941. We were four siblings: Ilonka, Vilmos (Volvi), Márjemka, and me, Miksa.

Ilonka got married in Vásárosnamény. Her husband was Samu Katz, and they had a men and women's ready-to-wear clothing store. They had three children: Imre, 17; Márta, 14; and Lacika, 11 years old. They were deported. No one came back.

Vilmos — his wife was Ella Glattstein from Mezöcsát. In Tokaj they had a fishing goods store, a comercial bag and string business, and commercial bags lending for farmers. They had two little daughters: Noémi, 10, and Juditka must have been 8 years old. They were deported. No one survived.

Márjemka — her husband was Sándor Friedlender. They lived in Tiszaluc. His business was live animal exporting. He shipped beef cattle to Italy. They had a little boy, Palika, who must have been 5-6 years old. Sándor disappeared as a labor battalion worker. Márjemka was deported with Palika. They didn't return.

Miksa, in the years before the war, was the representative for a Budapest chocolate and gourmet desserts company until April 1940 when he was called in for labor battalion service. After years of difficult and complicated forced labor, he survived and came back to Tokaj in January 1945. His wife, Ilonka Engel, likewise of Tokaj origin, had been deported with her parents and two sisters. The parents unfortunately perished in Auschwitz. Ilonka and her two sisters, Bözsike and Sárika, after horrible suffering returned to Tokaj in the summer of 1945. Ilonka and Miksa's wedding, February 12, 1946 was in Tokaj. Miksa opened up his grocery and sundries store and it was in operation until the summer of 1951 when they nationalized it and offered him a position in a state store. Ilonka made sweaters on a knitting machine and taught private students how to sew. After the October 1956 Revolution, they were successful in escaping in December into Austria, and in the beginning of 1957 they arrived in America. They settled in New Jersey. Miksa got a job in an aluminum door and window factory. Ilonka sewed and designed dresses. The children were enrolled in school. Some months later the family left New Jersey and moved to Pasadena, California. The children continued their studies. Miksa worked in an aluminum workshop for a few months. Afterwards, he opened up his own workshop (Aluminum Screen and Door Products Company). After 22 years, he sold it and retired. Ilonka went back to school and obtained her teacher's credential. The Pasadena City College employed her where she taught for 20 years tailoring and dress design. They have two children, both of whom created very nice careers: Henry and Márta.

Aunt Lotti was the next Billitzer girl. Her husband was Moric Fuchs, my father Henrik Fuchs's younger brother. They lived in Homona and had a firewood and coal business. Lotti néni died at the end of the 1920's. They had three girls: Jolánka, Olga, and Manci. Jolánka got married in Kézmárok and her husband was a tailor. I don't remember his name. Uncle Moric with the two girls were deported and they didn't come back.

Aunt Eszti —her husband was Jenö Haiman. They lived in Forro-Encse. They had a grocery store and he leased land and had a farm. They had a farm-wagon and horse and buggy for the farming. Uncle Jenö's mother and two older sisters also lived with them and they ran the grocery store. They had two daughters, Olga and Margit (Vityke), and five sons: Ire, Eizik, Pimbi, Zélig, and Mánele (Elek). Olga as a young girl got married. Her husband was Ignác Löwy. They lived in Forro-Encse. They had an oil warehouse and gas station. They had two little boys whose names I can't remember. Ire, Eszti néni's oldest son, also married. He took the daughter of a Debrecen printer and became partners in the business. Eizik studied tombstone engraving and ran his own factory up until deportation. Pimbi worked in a produce warehouse. Mánele was going to school. Eszti néni died in 1938, and Uncle Jenö remarried to Aunt Ilonka, a Miskolc woman who had a well-run printing shop. Uncle Jenö took it over and continued to work successfully.

Vityke, the youngest daughter, was situated by Uncle Jenö into a drugstore in Forro-Encsen. The store didn't do so well. She sold it and went up to Budapest and became partners in a similar store. She married and a little boy, Gyuri, was born. Her husband's name was Lövinger, and he disappeared as a labor battalion worker. Vityke gave up the drugstore and opened up a cosmetology salon in Budapest. She lived through the war in a "safe" house in Budapest with her son. After the war she re-opened her cosmetology salon. Some years later she gave it up and emigrated with her son to Australia, to Sydney. She continued the cosmetology salon in Sydney. Her son learned auto assembly and repair. At the end of the 1980's Vityke moved down to Florida. Her son Gyuri married and remained in Sydney.

The entire Haiman family was deported or was drafted into labor battalions. Those who lived through the Holocaust were Vityke with her son, Olga and her husband Löwy (their two little boys perished), and Mánele (Elek). The Löwys, soon after the end of the war, emigrated to New York and opened up a kosher restaurant in Brooklyn. Meanwhile, Elek also settled in New York and married. He studied the art of cooking and works in a restaurant as a chef. The rest of the members of the Haiman family all perished. This information goes back to 1958 when we lived in New Jersey and we visited them in New York. What is happening with them now I don't know, because we moved to California and all connections were broken.

Aunt Paula was the youngest Billitzer girl. Her husband, Markus Strasser, was the son of the Tokaj Rabbi, Akiba Strasser. He was likewise a rabbi. After the death of the Billitzer grandfather, the Jewish community of Szepesófalu selected him to be the rabbi. He filled this position there for many years until a larger Jewish community, Vágselye, asked him to be rabbi for a rabbinical position that opened up, which he accepted and occupied until deportation. They had no children. They were deported and perished.

Uncle Józsi was the only male member of the Billitzer family. He often visited us in Tokaj. I must have been 6-7 years old as far as I can recall. He was an older gentleman and sickly. He constantly smoked cigarettes and coughed. He didn't have a beard but he was very religious. There was always a book in his hand and he was reading, I think studying. As a child I always looked up to him with great respect. I remember that my father said that Uncle Jozsi was a great "Talmud-chochem", a great Talmud scholar. He even wrote a book, a copy of which is in my possession. The title of the book is Ele Hamicves, These are the Commandandments, and is written in Hebrew. The book is about the 613 laws that are required of every Jew to obey, the meaning of which he expounds upon. He lived in Szepesófalu at Aunt Paula's. He never married. I don't know when he died; I think toward the end of the 1920's.

I believe with this I have finished the history of the descendants of this branch of the Billitzer family, according to the best of my knowledge. I tried to write it down briefly, and I didn't go into small details. I imagine that someday one of the members of the family will continue to describe the family's subsequent history.

* *

Dad's first labor battalion in Szond, Hungary, Summer 1941

Top row: (fourth through seventh from left): Dad, his brother Vilmos, Bandi Klein, Icus Wassermann (Gyula *bácsi's* brother), and Sanyi Frankel

Bandi Klein was Lipot Klein's son. They had a tavern across from the Temple. Sanyi Frankel was from Tarcal and had a camera with which this photograph was taken.

All the men in the top row except Sanyi Frankel were from Tokaj. Joska Löwy, Lajcsi's father, was also in this group but not in this photograph.

My friend Isaac Guttman was not in this group, only in the later one. He was in a Yeshiva in Szatmár and from there was taken to another group first.

There was also a Berkowits boy. Weinberger was the stepfather. Both were *sochets*, ritual slaughterers, and *chazans,* cantors. Weinberger's second wife had two sons. The older one was Zacharia Berkowits who somehow got out to Switzerland before the war.

Recommended Resources

1. Berger, Alan L. & Naomi Berger. *Second Generation Voices: Reflections by Children of Holocaust Survivors and Perpetrators.* Syracuse, NY: Syracuse University Press, 2001.
2. Berger, Alan L. *Children of Job: American Second-Generation Witnesses to the Holocaust.* Albany, NY: State University of New York Press, 1997.
3. Braham, Randolph L. and Scott Miller. *The Nazis' Last Victims: The Holocaust in Hungary.* Detroit, MI: Wayne State University Press, 2002.
4. Braham, Randolph I. *The Politics of Genocide: The Holocaust in Hungary.* Detroit, MI: Wayne State University Press, 2000.
5. Epstein, Helen. *Children of the Holocaust: Conversations with Sons and Daughters of Survivors.* NY: Penguin, 1988.
6. Epstein, Helen. *Where She Came From: A Daughter's Search for Her Mother's History.* NY: Little, Brown, & Co, 1997.
7. Fenyvesi, Charles. *When the World Was Whole.* NY: Viking Penguin, 1990.
8. Fogelman, Eva. *Conscience and Courage: Rescuers of Jews During the Holocaust.* NY: Anchor, 1995.
9. Gilbert, Martin. *The Righteous: The Unsung Heroes of the Holocaust.* NY: Henry Holt, 2003.
10. Hass, Aaron. *In the Shadow of the Holocaust: The Second Generation.* NY: Cambridge University Press, 1996.

11. Hilberg, Raul. *Perpetrators Victims Bystanders: The Jewish Catastrophe 1933-1945.* NY: HarperCollins, 1992.
12. Hoffman, Eva. *After Such Knowledge: Memory, History, and the Legacy of the Holocaust.* NY: Public Affairs, 2004.
13. Langer, Lawrence L. *Holocaust Testimonies: The Ruins of Memory.* New Haven, CT: Yale University Press, 1991.
14. Lyman, Darryl. *Holocaust Rescuers: Ten Stories of Courage.* NY: Enslow, 1999.
15. Oliner, Samuel P. & Pearl M. Oliner. *The Altruistic Personality: Rescuers of Jews in Nazi Europe.* NY: Free Press, 1988.
16. Paldiel, Mordecai. *Sheltering the Jews: Holocaust Rescuers.* Kitchener, Ontario: Fortress Press, 1996.
17. Spiegelman, Art. *Maus: A Survivor's Tale. Volume I: My Father Bleeds History. Volume II: And Here My Troubles Began.* NY: Pantheon Books, 1973, 1986.
18. Wiesel, Elie. *After the Darkness: Reflections on the Holocaust.* NY: Schocken Books, 2002.

http://www.yadvashem.org.il/
Yad Vashem: The Holocaust Martyrs' and Heroes' Rememberance Authority

http://www3sympatico.ca/mighty1/
Women and the Holocaust: A Cyberspace of Their Own

http://www.ushmm.org/
United States Holocaust Memorial Museum

http://www.tauberholocaustlibrary.org/
The Tauber Holocaust Library and Education Program (formerly known as Holocaust Center of Northern CA)

http://www.genshoah.org/
Generations of the Shoah International

Acknowledgments

I am forever grateful to my parents and aunts Bözsi *néni* and Sárika *néni* for sharing both the joyful and painful experiences of their lives. In the midst of relating accounts of unthinkable inhumanity, their generosity and loving kindness helped sustain my spirit and strenghtened my determination to tell their stories.

Thank you to wonderful friends and colleagues who took an interest in this project and gave valuable feedback. Special thanks to Earlene Hass, Barbara Lewis, Irene and David McPhail, Joyce Ahern, Beth Burstein, Judith Skinner, Shelley Fields, Amy Rosenthal, and Julia Epstein; the Bay Area Independent School Librarians group, especially Brenda Brown, for encouragement and awarding me their annual Professional Development Grant; my colleagues at Drew School in San Francisco, especially Sam Cuddeback, III, for his generous support and vote of confidence; Dr. Jon Herzenberg for spirited discussions and opportunity to speak in his psychology classes; and Jennifer Weiser for her technological wizardry and artistic sensibility. *Köszönom* to Viktória Erdös, who happens to live with her family in our old house in Tokaj, for assistance in translating correspondence.

Ongoing gratitude and love go to my brother Henry, his children Sam and Miriam, and to my children Jacob and Sophie who make my heart sing. It has been sheer pleasure to share several journeys (and lots of *mákos*) back to our Jewish and Hungarian roots in Tokaj.

stork flying over the Tisza River

Tokaj, 2011

photo by Henry

Dad in front of his lemon tree

The Torah adorned with a crown of fresh flowers made by Mom and friends in honor of Shavuos

Pasadena, 1999, Erev Shavuos

photo by Kathy Kobayashi

Marta Fuchs was born in Budapest and lived in Tokaj until she escaped with her family to the U.S. in the wake of the Hungarian Revolution of 1956. She is a professional librarian and Director of Library Services at Drew School in San Francisco, CA and a licensed Marriage & Family Therapist in private practice in Albany, CA. For over two decades, Marta has spoken about Zoltán Kubinyi in temples, churches, interfaith programs, and schools. She can be contacted at legacyofrescue@gmail.com.

Proceeds from the sale of this book will be donated to the Morton & Ilona E. Fuchs Award at Pasadena Jewish Temple & Center in Pasadena, CA. The award gives recognition to B'nai Mitzvah students for devotion to their studies, service to the Temple, and *tikkun olam*, repairing the world though community service.

To make a contribution to the Fuchs Award, please contact the Pasadena Jewish Temple & Center, (626) 798- 1161, 1434 North Altadena Drive, Pasadena, California 91107, www.pjtc.net.